WITHDRAWN

D0087662

949.742 A573
Andric, Ivo, 1892-1975
The development of spiritual
life in Bosnia under the
influence of Turkish rule
48760

The Development of Spiritual Life in Bosnia under the Influence of Turkish Rule

949.742
A573

9-27-98

37.95

048760

The Development of Spiritual Life in
Bosnia under the Influence of Turkish Rule

Ivo Andrić

Želimir B. Juričić and John F. Loud,
Editors and Translators

Duke University Press Durham and London 1990

© 1990 Duke University Press
All rights reserved
Printed in the United States of America
on acid-free paper ∞
Library of Congress Cataloging-in-Publication Data
appear on the last page of this book.

Contents

Introduction

Ivo Andrić's formal education began in the summer of 1899 when, at the age of seven, he entered school in Višegrad, a colorful provincial town in southeastern Bosnia. Small and poorly equipped, the Višegrad elementary school (now the Vuk Karadžić school) was the only school in town. Situated beside the wooden bridge on the Rzav River, it was attended by some forty to fifty children from the town and its surrounding settlements. Its student body reflected the diverse demographic composition of the area: Poles, Jews, Muslims, Czechs, Germans, and Italians. On his way to and from school Andrić had to cross both the Drina and the Rzav bridges and walk through the main town. There is no doubt that the Višegrad bridge and the masterfully embroidered tales about it, which were narrated on the bridge itself—focal point of the town's life—by the town elders and passing travelers, had more than a passing effect on the mind of the future writer.

In the summer of 1903, after completing the Višegrad elementary school and with a yearly stipend of 200 Kronen from the Croatian society Napredak, Andrić moved to Sarajevo. There for the next eight years he attended the Velika Sarajevska Gimnazija (Great Sarajevo Gymnasium) and published his first poetic pieces. In October 1912, again with a scholarship from Napredak, he moved to Zagreb, Croatia's capital, where he entered the university. In his first year he studied biology, human anatomy, zoology, plant physiology, and mechanics as well as Croatian literature, which was taught by a well-known professor and politician, Dr. Đuro Šurmin. In the fall of 1913 Andrić moved to Austria to continue his studies at the University of Vienna. The shift in his interests from science to humanities is evident from his second-year transcript. Notable were his increasing interest in Serbian and Croatian literatures and the peoples of the Balkan

peninsula; teaching these subjects in Vienna were the foremost Sla-
vists of the period, Milan Rešetar and Joseph Jireček.[1]

Andrić's stay in Vienna was short. Unable to bear the severe
Austrian climate, which seriously affected his delicate health—inflam-
mation of the throat and lungs—Andrić moved to Poland on the
advice of his physician. In April 1914 he enrolled in the third year of
Arts at the University of Cracow. The physical and cultural climate of
the city seems to have agreed with the young student. "The place
suited me, I was in good spirits. The magnificent history of the Poles,
uttered through thousands of voices, the peace radiating from the city,
the people . . . , the kind friends who ardently discussed the freedom
of their homeland, the respected professors whose lectures I attended. . . . Cracow is the only place in Europe—and I have known quite a
few!—whose memories and name can stir my heart and warm my
blood."[2]

Following the assassination in 1914 of the Austrian archduke,
Franz Ferdinand, in Sarajevo, Andrić interrupted his studies and hur-
riedly left Poland. However, upon his arrival in what is now Yugo-
slavia he was arrested, imprisoned, and then interned for his alleged
participation in a revolutionary movement known as "Mlada Bosna,"
which opposed the Hapsburg regime and sought unity and independence for the South Slavic peoples. He was released in 1917 at the age
of twenty-two, in poor health and financially desperate. He worked
feverishly at his writing and to augment his income took a part-time
editorial position with a local literary journal. In 1918 he registered into
the final year of his studies at Zagreb University, but because of health,
family, and financial problems he was forced to leave, having com-
pleted the required course work but not having taken the final exams.
With a view to securing some kind of steady employment, he wrote to
Tugomir Alaupović, his former teacher at secondary school and now a
cabinet minister in the newly formed Kingdom of Serbs, Croats, and
Slovenes, with the following plea:

> My mother lives with my aunt and uncle in Višegrad. They do not
> live badly and if I send them anything it is out of affection, but the
> uncle is 67 years old, with one foot in the grave, and the day he
> dies the sacred and hard duty to take care of my mother and aunt
> will fall to me. It is because of this that I am no longer inclined to

continue living this poor, if free and nice, life. I do not have anyone to discuss this matter with, and thus I beg you to keep my situation in mind and help me with your influence and advice. My only desire is that my job not turn me completely away from literary activity. Please forgive me for talking so much about myself and my troubles, but it is a question of my relatives about whom it is already my duty to be concerned.[3]

Alaupović readily offered his former student a junior position in his ministry (the Ministry of Religious Affairs), which Andrić accepted. In October 1919 the twenty-seven-year-old future government employee took up residence in Belgrade, a city which, like Cracow, impressed him from the start and which would make him its lifelong devotee.

Andrić's tenure at the Ministry of Religious Affairs was brief. In February 1920 he was granted a transfer to the more prestigious Ministry of Foreign Affairs. Soon he was posted as a vice-consul in the Royal Yugoslav Consulate in the Vatican. He found work in the consulate less taxing than he expected. This allowed him to devote more time to his other pursuits and literary work. In his year and a half stay in the capital of Roman Catholicism, Andrić did a fair amount of writing and sightseeing. In September, "Put Alije Đerzeleza" (The Journey of Đerzelez Alija), his first short story, was published in Belgrade. "Ćorkan i Švabica" (Ćorkan and the German Woman), another story with a Bosnian theme, was also submitted for publication. Surrounded by some of the world's greatest art treasures and the spectacular scenic beauty of the country, the young diplomat found time to explore local museums and archives, also taking in the cultural and historic sites with which Italy, and the holy city of Rome, abounded. In the next two years he was transferred twice, first to Bucharest, Romania, in 1921 and a year later, now as vice-consul second class, to the Royal Yugoslav Consulate in the small town of Trieste on the Yugoslav-Italian border. As his health deteriorated almost immediately after his arrival in Italy—catarrh, causing anemia and weakness, was discovered in both his lungs—he begged the ministry for yet another transfer. In January 1923, after a brief vacation in Venice, Andrić left Italy for the second time. In his long diplomatic career, which officially spanned more than two decades, he never returned to that country. His work in the consulate in Graz was light. This allowed him to devote more time to his writing and to honor a number of long-standing commitments to the Yugoslav journals (*Jugoslavenska Njiva, Srpski Književni Glasnik, Savremenik*) and publishers (Cvijanović) besieging him for contributions. Then, at the end of 1923, just as he was beginning to settle into his new post and his writing was gaining recognition, he suddenly found himself unemployed. Still an unfinished student of Slavistics, Andrić was directly affected by a new government regulation concerning qualifications of civil service personnel. The regulation stated, in part, that only persons with recognized university degrees would be permitted to continue occupying important positions in the kingdom's civil service, particularly in the diplomatic services abroad (Article 243, Royal Proclamation No. 5633, 1923).[4] Andrić was requested to surrender his position as vice-consul in Graz and to leave the service. He was offered two months' severance pay.[5]

A number of appeals aimed at circumventing the new regulations and retaining Andrić in the service were immediately made to the ministry in Belgrade: two by Vladislav Budisavljević, the consul-general in Graz and Andrić's immediate superior, and one by Andrić himself. In his first letter to Momčilo Ninčić, the Yugoslav foreign minister, Budisavljević praised Andrić's dedication to work and his exemplary behavior both at and outside the workplace and cited his very good rapport with his colleagues, characteristics deserving of consideration before the final decision was made regarding his dismissal. "I, personally, would wish Andrić to stay in this Consulate, if at all possible," he concluded.[6] In his second letter Budisavljević mentioned Andrić's exceptional dedication to, and his thorough knowledge of, all aspects of diplomatic work, his noted qualifications and reputation as a writer, as well as his knowledge of the German language, which Budisavljević considered absolutely essential. He requested Ninčić to allow Andrić to remain with the consulate at least until the completion of his doctoral studies, which he had begun one year before, in 1923, at the University of Graz. "It is my firm belief that with time Andrić will prove himself worthy of your trust and will become an excellent civil servant, who can only be a credit to our profession, the country, and its people."[7]

Andrić wrote his own appeal to the minister: "I request the Ministry to keep me as a day worker in the Royal Consulate in Graz, with my present income, until I have finished my doctorate. Should this be possible, I am prepared to forfeit the severance pay promised me."[8]

At the end of February 1924 the minister made his decision. Andrić was to remain in the consulate as a day worker until completion of his doctoral studies. Until further notice he was to be paid his present salary as vice-consul (second class), abroad.[9] Having thus temporarily settled his working status, and with it his financial situation, Andrić now turned his full attention to completing his university studies. These included writing a doctoral dissertation, passing two very rigorous examinations, and finishing the required course work.

Would Andrić have undertaken this most challenging and demanding task under different circumstances? Probably not, according to his own subsequent assessment of the situation: "I was under the compulsion of the new civil service law. The law had to be obeyed then as well. By the new civil service law a complete university education was required for my position in the Ministry. Thus I temporarily left the service."[10]

According to Andrić's "Record of Degree Program," the *Index*, listing the courses taken by a student, the hours of attendance, and the names of professors conducting them, in his two semesters at the University of Graz he attended a total of thirty-nine hours of lectures ranging from history, language, and grammar to sociology and philosophy. Specifically, in the winter semester of 1923 he took the following courses:

History of Austria after 1848
    (2 hours, Dr. R. Kaindl)
Seminar in Austrian History
    (2 hours, Kaindl)
Introduction to the Study of Slavic Philology
    (2 hours, Dr. H. F. Schmid)
Old Church Slavonic Grammar
    (4 hours, Schmid)
Exercises in Old Church Slavonic
    (2 hours, Schmid)
The Concept of Individuality in the Philosophy of Nature and
    Philosophical Sociology
    (1 hour, Dr. Spitzer)[11]

For the summer semester, April–July 1924, Andrić's transcript reads as follows:

Historical Grammar of the Russian Language
    (4 hours, Schmid)
Slavic Antiquities
    (2 hours, Schmid)
Seminar in Slavic Philology
    (3 hours, Schmid)
History of Austria since 1848, Part 2
    (5 hours, Kaindl)
Little Germans and Great Germans
    (1 hour, Kaindl)
History Seminar
    (2 hours, Kaindl)
Theory of Perception, Part 2
    (4 hours, Dr. E. Mally)
Seminar in Philosophy
    (2 hours, Mally)[12]

In addition to lectures, doctoral candidates were required to pass two extensive oral examinations based on the required courses and on their own area of research. They were permitted to take these examinations only after submitting their doctoral dissertations, which were then evaluated by a panel of readers and duly marked. In other words, the dissertation held the key to one's studies toward the doctoral degree.

Andrić submitted his dissertation to the office of the Dean of the Faculty of Philosophy on 14 May 1924. It was officially received the next day and almost at once forwarded for assessment to Professors Schmid and Kaindl. Heinrich Felix Schmid and Raimund Friedrich Kaindl had been selected by the office of the dean as the most competent scholars in Andrić's special field of interest, which was Bosnia. Their appraisal is given below after a description and summary of the work itself.

Its title (page 1) reads *Die Entwicklung des geistigen Lebens in Bosnien unter der Einwirkung der türkischen Herrschaft* (The Development of Spiritual Life in Bosnia under the Influence of Turkish Rule). Above it are the signatures of the two readers (Schmid and Kaindl) together with the number of the dissertation, the date of its submission, and the stamp of the Faculty of Philosophy of the Karl Franz University in Graz. Page 2 reads, "Dissertation for the granting of the doctorate of the Faculty of Philosophy of the Karl Franz University in Graz, presented by Ivo Andrić from Sarajevo, SHS [Kingdom of Serbs, Croats, and Slovenes]." The body of the work consists of 143 double-spaced typewritten pages and is divided into two parts: volume 1 (marked by hand as "Bd. 1"), 107 pages, constituting the text itself, and volume 2 ("Bd. 2"), thirty-six pages, consisting of notes to the separate chapters (*Anmerkungen*). The work is framed by a Preface (*Vorwort*) and a Supplement (*Anhang*).

In his brief, one-page preface the author states what he proposes doing: "to trace the evolution of Bosnia's intellectual and spiritual life from the time of national independence to the final disappearance of Turkish power." He also offers the following disclaimer: "Individual segments along the line of development cannot all be traced with equal clarity and force. Even in Bosnia itself, sources for many events and many a stretch of time are lacking or else unreliable. Working outside the country, I have had to content myself with those at hand, or with such as I was able to procure while assembling this work." The Preface concludes, succinctly and significantly: "In content and basic idea the present treatment is related to other works that I have composed in a different form and on a different occasion." Andrić referred here no doubt to the short fiction on Bosnian themes that he had already published, including such well-known stories as "Put Alije Đerzeleza," "Ćorkan i Švabica," "U musafirhani," and "Mustafa Madžar." (Seven of these were to appear as a collection during the very year of his degree, 1924.) It is entirely possible that Andrić incorporated into his dissertation much material that he had accumulated over the years from the archives and libraries of the three Franciscan monasteries in Bosnia—Kreševo, Fojnica, and Sutjeska—and that he had intended to use in the writing of his "great Franciscan drama."[13] Unfortunately, that drama never saw the light of day. The fact that Andrić was able to write his dissertation in a relatively short period of time—less than a year—only adds to speculation that his thesis material was drawn from a supply earmarked for literary purposes and that, skillful craftsman as he already was with the pen, he had no difficulty in molding it into presentable form for a scholarly dissertation. Some passages still exude that unmistakable Andrićevan short-story flavor, however carefully disguised in scholarly garb. But let us now turn to the work itself.

Chapter 1 examines spiritual life in Bosnia before the Turkish conquest in 1463. Of its three sections, the first analyzes Bosnia's general level of culture during its independence, the second considers the roles of the three churches—Catholic, Orthodox, and Patarin—in the country's cultural and political development up to the conquest, while the third deals with spiritual and political conditions in the country just prior to its being invaded.

The relatively short second chapter is concerned with the most characteristic reforms implemented by the Turkish occupiers. Islam, the religion of a warring Asiatic nation, in Andrić's analysis spread with unusual rapidity in Bosnia. Although it was diametrically op-posed to the three dominant faiths battling for supremacy on Bosnian soil, Islam—which had been born and grew to maturity in a foreign climate and under a different social order and resisted change of any description—quickly suppressed the spiritual life of Bosnia. It was land and property that chiefly motivated the Bosnian nobility to con-vert to Islam. Besides religion, another alien custom brought by the conqueror and imposed on Bosnia was the child-tribute. Bright, good-looking, and healthy Christian boys aged from ten to fifteen and gathered from all parts of the empire were taken by force from their homes and carried to "Stambol." There they were circumcised, con-verted, made to forget their country of origin, and trained to serve either in the ranks of the janissaries or introduced into the governing elite. Some of these recruits eventually emerged as the highest military administrators and commanders in the Ottoman armies, and a select few even rose to the supreme post of grand vizier. Bosnia was not spared from the child-tribute. Andrić, some twenty years after finish-ing his dissertation, was to elaborate on this strange, merciless Turkish institution of the Adžami-Oglan in his novel *The Bridge on the Drina (Na Drini ćuprija)*.

The central, third chapter is the longest and most important part of the dissertation and divides the work into equal parts. Here are examined the social and administrative organizations established by the Turks and the influence that they exerted on the lives of the *rayah*, the non-Muslims, in Bosnia. The law governing non-Islamic peoples generally throughout the empire was known as the *Kanun-i-Rayah* (*rayah* law code). It consisted of a series of ordinances, authoritative decrees that nonbelievers, particularly Christians and Jews, were expected to follow and obey without question. Andrić lists twenty-four such regulations and proceeds to show both how unequally they were enforced in Bosnia and how deeply they cut into the moral and economic fabric of life for nonbelievers. He maintains that the Turkish, and particularly the local Islamized, ethnically Slavic, elements hindered any social or cultural uplifting of the *rayah*. They resisted and fought against all reforms and saw in each cultural achievement of the "infidel" *rayah* a tendency undermining the existing order and a danger to their own rights and privileges. Such attitudes were bound to have a negative effect on the literary and cultural life of the non-Muslim populations. This is the subject of the following chapter.

Divided into two parts, chapter 4 describes the intellectual life of the Catholic population under the Turks, as manifested in the literary and cultural work of the Franciscans. The first part deals with the purely religious literature of the seventeenth and eighteenth centuries, the second with the literature of the nineteenth century. The Turkish occupation of Bosnia caused not only the collapse of the Bosnian kingdom but also of the Catholic church as a bastion of Western interests in the country. Most of the Franciscan monasteries and rectories were destroyed and the order was persecuted: of the original thirty-two monasteries only a few remained (Kreševo, Sutjeska, Fojnica, and Olovo) to keep *"das geistige Leben"* alive during the four long centuries of Turkish oppression. The literature of the Bosnian Franciscans was not the literature of idle, isolated, rich, and learned monks with refined and learned purposes. Rather primitive and at its early stages unoriginal and unstructured, the literature of the Bosnian Franciscans served as best it could the spiritual needs of a wide segment of the Christian population under the most difficult of circumstances and at the time it was needed most. This is "one of its most beautiful qualities and at the same time one of its greatest merits," the author concludes.

In the fifth and final chapter of the dissertation Andrić discusses the status of the Serbian Orthodox church under Turkish hegemony and especially during the first century of their rule. After a brief examination of such topics as church organization, living conditions for the clergy, the significance of monasteries to the Orthodox population, Greek influence on the Orthodox church in Serbia (and by extension Bosnia), early literary attempts, and the printing or copying of the first church books, the author concludes that the Serbian Orthodox church in Bosnia during the time of Turkish rule could not develop its energies toward the outside. Its clergy produced no literary works like those of the Franciscans. Spiritually, the church drew its strength as much from folk songs as it did intellectually from church books; the former were as deeply rooted in the peasant heart as the latter.

Besides the Preface and the five main chapters, there are two additional parts to Andrić's thesis: a short three and one-half page Supplement, and the thirty-six pages of Notes.

In the Supplement he briefly discusses the little-known subject of hybrid literature, that is, the attempts by Bosnian Muslims to write poetry in the Serbo-Croatian language but in Arabic script. These attempts extended from the seventeenth to the nineteenth centuries. The number of poems under consideration is small—seventeen poems by eleven poets—and their qualitative importance low, for the language is misformed and pressed into a foreign poetic mold, the rhyme nearly always false, and the verse for the most part saturated with Turkish borrowings. Nonetheless, the poems were deemed deserving of consideration as a concrete example of the influence of oriental on Slavic culture.

The Notes to the five chapters illustrate the wide variety of native and foreign sources (German, French, Latin, Italian, and Russian) that were consulted and used by the author. These include original monastery and church documents and books (many written by hand), chronicles, rare books, newspapers and journals, and reminiscences by foreign visitors to Bosnia, both early and late, as for example the English scientist George Wheler and the Turkish traveler Evlija-Effendi, or the nineteenth-century writers Asbóth and Rośkiewicz.

On 14 May 1924 Andrić submitted his dissertation with a request for evaluation. Within a week of receiving the work its two examiners, Professors Schmid and Kaindl, recommended in a four-page, handwritten report that it be accepted as submitted and that its author be permitted to proceed with the final phase of his studies, that is, to take the candidacy examinations in the subjects relevant to his field of research. The compulsory examinations, or *"strenge Prüfungen,"* con-

rial, particularly in the contemporary area, was not as extensive as it could have been. This stemmed from his heavy reliance on sources close at hand, primarily those at the university and city libraries in Graz. Although well stocked with post-1900 Slavic sources, these libraries experienced very serious gaps in such areas as the pre-1900 Bulgarian writings about the Patarins and original Turkish sources on Bosnia. Second, Andrić had neglected to consult the original foreign sources. Whether for financial, linguistic, or other reasons, he was often compelled to rely on translations, fragmentary and questionable, and this contributed to the simplicity of some of his conclusions and judgments. The lack of a bibliography, even a synoptic one (there are only notes to chapters), disproportion in the length of the chapters (some are double, even triple, the length of others), and the absence of a concluding chapter (the last "chapter" is the one on hybrid literature, a new topic and not a summation)—all were cited by Schmid and Kaindl as further shortcomings. Although the readers found these to be minor faults, their rectification was thought essential if the dissertation were to be published. The Seminar for Slavic Philology in the Faculty of Philosophy in Graz was suggested as a possible place of publication.

And yet Andrić's dissertation was never published in its author's lifetime. We can only speculate on the reasons. It could be that he considered his literary work more important and profitable: the first collection of his short stories had already appeared in 1924, and some of the short stories also began to come out in foreign publications. This not only helped him financially but advanced his rapidly growing literary career as a writer. His uncle-guardian Ivan Matkovčik died in Višegrad in 1924; his mother (she died a year later in Sarajevo) was seriously ill. Under these circumstances it would have been more difficult for the thirty-two-year-old Andrić to carry on with his research in Bulgaria and Turkey, as his readers advised. More than anything else he was simply saturated with academic work, work which he found extremely strenuous and demanding but not very rewarding. "Two days ago I received my doctorate at the University here," he wrote to a friend in Zagreb. "I put a great deal of time and energy into this work. Now I should think of doing something more sensible."[15]

Examined through modern eyes, Andrić's dissertation has a number of structural and technical deficiencies. These, however, do not diminish its significance. Written more than sixty years ago, when he was just starting as a writer, this scholarly document is permeated with topics that Andrić the writer in one form or another incorporated into his mature literary prose. The thesis, based on academic research, is by Andrić the scholar; Andrić the storyteller employed the same facts in fictionalized form, treading lightly across the line separating facts from fiction and back again without pedantically marking the difference. For in Andrić's works romance and scholarship are unconscious allies, not enemies.

Central to both dissertation and artistic prose is Bosnia, the land in which Andrić was born and was schooled and where the fate of the Balkans has so often been decided. Whereas the Bosnia of his dissertation is a land of dry statistics, factual historic events, and countless names and personalities, in his fiction that same Bosnia becomes imbued with life, a sort of writer's experimental laboratory for observing human behavior and the bewildering turns and twists of history and for reflecting on life in general. In his prose, in fact, Andrić is never far from the most thorough historical research. He is at his best when the historian walks hand in hand with the storyteller. There is no substitute for his minute description of scenes, which his scholarship bases on a confident mastery of every significant detail, be it an execution or the technicalities of medieval bridge building as in *The Bridge on the Drina*. Bosnia was not chosen accidentally either as the theme of his doctoral research or as the locale for many stories and novels. This land was in his blood long before he became a scholar and writer. "I should call Bosnia my spiritual home, and when you call a place by that name, you have admitted everything."[16]

Besides Bosnia, there are a number of other features that are common to both the dissertation and Andrić's artistic prose. The epic canvas, the feeling that events are flowing rather than progressing, the lack of shape, or rather the shape of the events themselves, their chronological sequencing, the gruesomeness of some events, the ability to compress history into narrow, local surroundings and give it general human value, cameo techniques rather than the deep psychological soundings of his heroes, the deep-seated hatred and conflicts among the Muslims, Turks, Serbs, and Jews on the regional level, and war-tormented Europe on the wider stage, the communicative and informative, yet clear, mode of expression, are all elements common to

Editorial Note

The present edition and translation of Andrić's doctoral thesis departs from the format of the manuscript as he left it: the notes, which originally made up a separate fascicle, are repositioned in abbreviated and edited form at the end of the book, and an annotated list of works cited has been added to the whole. To the dissertation's first two readers the lack of a bibliography was a minor deficit of historical scholarship. However, to scholars of Andrić today, a bibliography gives access to the written sources of major historical fiction.

This translation of the German original closely follows the typewritten, archival copy kept in the University of Graz library without attempting to reproduce its every feature. (Specialists are referred to the bilingual edition earlier issued by the Andrić Foundation in *Sveske* I, no. 1 [Belgrade: Zadužbina Ive Andrića, 1982]). Marginal comments, for example, by his two advisors are omitted; emphasis (italic typeface) is preserved only for typed (not penciled) underlining; paragraphing proceeds by logical content rather than by the choppy, journalistic style—often one sentence per paragraph—favored in the original, legal-size manuscript; and headers and subheaders have been added for ease of reference. Andrić's own preferences, however, have been followed consistently in the case of proper nouns: for example, Ragusa for "Dubrovnik," Patarin for "Bogomil," and Constantinople for "Carigrad" or even "Istanbul." Whatever is in parentheses was parenthetical in the manuscript. Brackets enclose editorial clarifications or additions, such as alternative or modern place names, translations of occasional passages in Latin and Italian, or minor factual errors to which attention is drawn by the use of [*sic*]. Dialect discrepancies are overlooked. In his notes the author's spelling and punctuation have been allowed to stand, as have his reliance on the roman (Croatian)

both Andrić's dissertation and his best prose work. Understandably, being a historical survey rather than a work of fiction, the dissertation lacks the sweep and velocity of the novel, its color and symbolism, its timeless effect, even while dealing with the same period and the same facts. There is as well Andrić's superb use of language. The impeccable craft and economy of organization that distinguish most of his narratives are characteristic also of his learned prose. Always in control as to choice and economy of words—not a word too few or too many— Andrić is as dignified, vivid, and natural here as in his fiction.

In many ways, then, Andrić's doctoral dissertation served a dual purpose. On the nonliterary front it was his union card, enabling him to retain his position in the diplomatic service and providing him with financial security. It also gave him a systematically researched body of historical information that he could use in his works of narrative prose. It will probably never be known why he hesitated to publish such an important and interesting document.[17]

alphabet as opposed to the cyrillic (Serbian, Russian) alphabet of some of his sources. The editors have expanded citations where necessary to clarify the relations between texts and sources.

The adjective *geistig*, which encompasses both "spiritual" and "intellectual" in English, has been rendered as "spiritual" in the title but elsewhere sometimes as the one, sometimes as the other (and occasionally as both), in keeping with shifting context.

The Development of Spiritual Life in Bosnia under the Influence of Turkish Rule

Preface

The conquest of Constantinople, it has been said, "dealt a wound to European man." Few countries could have taken that blow harder or felt it more deeply than Bosnia. In what follows a modest effort will be made to trace the evolution of Bosnia's intellectual and spiritual life from the time of national independence to the final disappearance of Turkish power.

Individual segments along the line of development cannot all be traced with equal clarity and force. Even in Bosnia itself, sources for many events and many a stretch of time are lacking or else unreliable. Working outside the country, I have had to content myself with those at hand, or with such as I was able to procure while assembling this work.

My description aims at bringing into relief the conditions created by Turkish hegemony, those by which its impact may be recognized. Accordingly, my focus has been on the attendant circumstances by which spiritual life was channeled and guided, circumstances hitherto little studied and known, rather than on specific literary monuments bearing the imprint of that life.

In content and basic idea the present treatment is related to other works that I have composed in a different form and on a different occasion.

1 Prologue: Spiritual Life in
Bosnia Before the Turkish Conquest

Bosnia's General Cultural Level

In order to grasp the significance of the Turkish invasion and its attendant circumstances for Bosnia's spiritual life, both when it took place and later, we must necessarily reflect briefly on religious life and its development in the country at the time of its independence.

The nature and kind of culture that existed in Bosnia during independence—in short, its cultural level just prior to the invasion—is a question repeatedly taken up in both Serbo-Croatian and non–Serbo-Croatian scholarship. A German researcher, Moriz Hoernes, has reasoned on the basis of his archaeological investigations that one can hardly talk of any culture in Bosnia during the Middle Ages.[1] For lack of other material, Hoernes draws his conclusions largely from Patarin tombstones and excavations. The rough, primitive aspect of their gravestone reliefs, the paucity of invention, and the absence of anything culturally distinctive in these chiseled stone figures all serve Hoernes as proof that Bosnia was culturally far behind its neighbors. From the monuments he concludes that "the Bosnian population was totally lacking in religious sense" and "completely barbaric." A number of grave site excavations that Hoernes carried out at various locations and that yielded neither weapons nor jewelry only strengthened his views.[2]

Among the Serbo-Croatian archaeologists of that period there were a few, though not of the first rank, who tried to refute Hoernes's argument by pointing out that "graves alone and the inscriptions on them scarcely constitute sufficient evidence to conclude anything about Bosnia's culture during her independence."[3] Others went still further, maintaining in diametric contrast to the position of Hoernes that these

very tombstones are "living and irrefutable signs of the cultural development, power and well-being of the people who erected them."[4]

Asbóth, in his well-known work on Bosnia, took the middle
ground on this issue.[5] In the reliefs of the Patarin gravestones he saw
the impact of late Romanesque stonemasons and at the same time "a
certain influence of Byzantine taste mediated by Greek rule and the
Greek church." We can infer, Asbóth concluded, from these insuffi-
cient remains "a very characteristic national culture rooted in the
national life and spirit and representing a truthful image of it, though
having registered—like every culture—outside influence as it grew."[6]

It is not the purpose of the present work to analyze and evaluate
this question more precisely. The intermediate position, however,
would appear to hew most closely to the historical truth. For although
there can be no doubt that the oriental origins and strong exclusivity of
the Patarin faith, like a mighty dam, impeded the penetration of
Western civilizing currents, on the other hand it can safely be assumed
also that Rome and Byzantium had their impact, as did the family
relationships and political connections of the Bosnian kings and nobility with the Serbian and Hungarian courts and, finally, the uninter-
rupted contact with Ragusa [Dubrovnik]. None of these could have
passed by without a trace. Nor, surely, could Bosnia's geographic
location or the condition of its roads, if hardly helpful to north-south
traffic, have actually blocked such influence.[7]

Not only the kings but numerous Bosnian magnates as well maintained constant and lively intercourse with Ofen [Buda] and Ragusa.[8]
They were honored with the highest decorations, participated at con-
vocations and tournaments. Presumably they had a certain degree of
"chivalric education and refinement." The mighty of Bosnia kept
houses in Ragusa. The one belonging to the voivode Sandalj Hranić,
as we know, was furnished in accordance with his personal instructions, and this was done with such taste that the house was imitated
by others in the city.[9] At the beginning of the fifteenth century *sona-
tores, ioculatores, buffones*, and a *lautarius* are mentioned at the court of
the king and in the houses of the nobility. The latter sent their actors to
Ragusa for celebrations and the townsfolk in turn sent their musicians
(*pifferi* and *tubete*).[10] Silk, finely woven materials, marinated fish and
the like were presented by the people of the town to members of the
court and to individual nobles.

A feeling for the gifts of a refined civilization, in short, was not entirely absent among the ruling class. Such contacts could not fail to influence the nobility's taste and general culture.[11]

Church Conditions in Bosnia

The Catholic Church

As early as the year 530 at the so-called First Council of Salona there was mention of a bishopric in Bosnia subordinate to the archbishop of Salona.[12] In the eleventh century this Bosnian bishopric was incorporated into the newly created church province of Antivari-Dioclea.[13] For a very brief period it came under the jurisdiction of the archbishop of Ragusa,[14] after which, in the year 1247, it was subordinated for good to the archbishopric of Kalocsa.[15] Thus Bosnia fell into total dependence, ecclesiastically, on Hungary. From that moment on the Catholic church and the political supremacy of Hungary came to be regarded as identical in Bosnia.

In 1344, at the time of Stjepan Kotromanić, there were three bishoprics in Bosnia: the Bosnian one, one of Duvno, and one of Makarska. Although Stjepan Kotromanić himself was of the Orthodox faith, he encouraged the spread of Catholicism by the Franciscans, "guided by purely political motives."[16] Also under Tvrtko I, who himself had converted from Orthodoxy to Catholicism, there existed religious tolerance for all three doctrines, at least for a time.[17]

Immediately after the death of Stjepan Dabiša (in 1395), however, inseparably linked to dissension within the nobility and coinciding with the first Turkish incursions, evil days closed in upon the Catholic church in Bosnia. The Patarins increased their numbers both among the nobility and the people as a whole, as well as at court. And even though the kings were on the side of the Catholic church, they were so disposed only for political reasons ("*fictus christianus*" [feigned Christian]).[18] Catholic churches were neglected and destroyed and the bishops of northern Bosnia, who had earlier moved their residence from Bosnia to Djakovo in Slavonia,[19] lost authority entirely in districts south of the River Sava. Church organization almost completely fell apart. All through the fifteenth century the Franciscans remained as the only defenders of the Catholic faith in Bosnia.[20]

Under the last two kings the church, despite all, rose to unheralded power and importance. Yet it was nothing more than the last gleam of splendor before sunset. General collapse was only accelerated by the hasty conversions of kings and nobles. The moral rupture and disunity of the Bosnian ruling classes and that of the Western powers from whom they desperately sought support were now exposed to full view.

King Stjepan Tomaš [1443–61] accepted the Catholic faith in 1444, a decision that delighted the pope,[21] and an orientation toward the West might also have been anticipated in the light of further events: the king divorced his wife, a Patarin, and married the daughter of the Grand Voivode Stjepan Vukčić, who agreed to the conversion of that same daughter to Catholicism, although he himself was a Patarin.[22] The example set by the king was soon followed by his nearest relatives and the most respected members of the Bosnian nobility. Among the first to take the Catholic faith was the king's brother, Radivoj. That was a sign of the times. It was this same Radivoj who, in the reign of Tvrtko II Tvrtković [1404–9; 1421–43], repeatedly led the Turks into Bosnia, plundering the country along with them.[23]

Even though the high nobility easily adjusted its religious convictions to its own interests, the bulk of the Bosnian people remained loyal to their "Bosnian church" and the Patarins continued to play a major role in public life. For instance, upon a complaint by the Franciscans that he had failed to persecute the Patarins, the king convinced the pope that they "could hardly be dislodged without jeopardizing the kingdom."[24] And when Stjepan Tomaš, succumbing to pressures from the pope and the Hungarian governor Hunyadi, later decreed that the Patarins should "either be baptized or emigrate," it was the beginning of the end. For this fateful decree resulted in the mass emigration of the Patarins into Hercegovina. There they came under the protection of the king's father-in-law, Stjepan Vukčić. And it was not long before they were all at each other's throats. In those endless battles King Stjepan Tomaš himself was slain in 1461. (According to a Croatian chronicle, he was killed by his own son, Stjepan Tomašević, and his brother, Radivoj.)[25]

Stjepan Tomašević carried on his father's ill-starred policy with even greater commitment, persecuting Patarins at the same time as fighting Turks.[26] In vain did the pope send the new king the crown as a sign of his favor; in vain did the king assume a title that had never before been bestowed on the kings of Bosnia.[27] The much provoked Patarins and the conquest-hungry Turks were near at hand, the pope far away and his help trivial. Hungary was jealous, the Catholic world indifferent. So it came about that both sides in their bitter mutual struggle only hastened the inevitable.

What was most characteristic of the growth and function of Catholicism within the kingdom of Bosnia was that it was spread by a foreign tongue, led by foreigners, and dependent upon foreign political and military might.

Strong colonies of Saxons (Hungarian Germans) and Dalmatian Romans, as well as inhabitants of Ragusa who had settled in cities and near mines either as miners or merchants, formed the centers of Catholic church life; here too were established the earliest monasteries (Olovo, Kreševo, Fojnica). Thus we find that the first organizers and representatives of the Catholic clergy were without exception foreigners (Fra Geraldo Odonis, Fra Peregrinus de Saxonia, etc.).[28] The language of the church remained, in spite of all difficulties, Latin. In the first place this enabled the church authorities to oversee the purity of the faith, as use of the vernacular would have readily invited contamination by the Patarin heresy and the Orthodox schism. Second, from the very start the Holy See was determined to nip in the bud any notion in Bosnia that religious services could possibly be conducted in a language other than Latin. Bosnia was to be safeguarded from the risk of an encounter between a Slavonic liturgy on the one hand and a Latin liturgy on the other—encounters such as had been occurring ever since the tenth century in the Croatian coastal regions.[29]

In the year 1203 we find the papal nuncio Johannes de Casamaris writing to Pope Innocent III as follows: "Noveritia praeterea, quod in regno de Bosnia non est nisi unus episcopatus et episcopus mode mortuus est. Si posset fieri quod aliquis *Latinus* ibi poneretur, etc." [There is this news besides: in the kingdom of Bosnia there exists but one bishopric and the bishop has recently died. If it be possible, let someone who is *Latin* be appointed there.][30] Ban Stjepan Kotromanić, through the Republic of Venice, asked Pope Clement IV in 1347 to send Bosnia only missionaries thoroughly conversant with Slavic ("or capable of acquiring it soon"), so that they might communicate with the people directly and also be able to instruct converts "in *Latin* grammar and the faith of the Roman church."[31] Two years before the collapse of the Bosnian kingdom, when with a cry of despair the last king, Stjepan Tomašević, appealed to the pope for help, he found it expedient to say that he had an advantage over his father (who was, to be sure, Catholic but only "newly converted") because he himself "had learned *Latin* and had embraced Christianity out of conviction." This he emphasized.[32]

When Pope Innocent III came to learn of a "great heresy" in Bosnia in 1199, he turned to the Hungarian king Emmerich, who was suzerain to the Bosnian ban, and requested that he "call the ban to account and forbid him to protect Patarins. Should the ban not obey, let the Hungarian king fall upon Bosnia with his troops in a surprise attack, deprive the Patarins of all their property and expel them, together with the ban."[33] From that moment to the collapse of the kingdom Bosnia was the stage for incessant wars in which the Hungarian kings, by supporting and protecting Catholicism, at the same time made good their claims to sovereign rights in the country. The two roles are frequently confused and identified, one with the other.

It is a remarkable coincidence that only under Turkish rule could the Catholic church—severely hobbled though it was—develop spontaneously and sink deeper roots.

The Serbian Orthodox Church

The history of the Serbian Orthodox church is no doubt the darkest point in Bosnia's religious life. Klaić takes as given that there were already in the eleventh century members of this confession in Bosnia, particularly in the eastern part of the country.[34] The only positive pieces of evidence we have are the fact that the Serbian king Stefan, son of Stefan Nemanja, had himself crowned in 1217 as "Stefan the Great, King and Ruler of all Serbian lands as well as of Dioclea [Zeta-Dioklitija], Dalmatia, Travunja [Travenia], and the diocese of Hum,"[35] and the fact that his brother, St. Sava, when putting the country's church affairs in order, installed the bishop of Hum with his seat in Ston in the year 1219. It is therefore quite likely that this bishop's sphere of influence extended to the utmost border of the Serbian state, that is, to the Narenta [the River Neretva]. But once the ban of Bosnia, Stjepan Kotromanić, resumed control over the Hum area in 1321, the Serbian Orthodox bishop had to withdraw from Ston.[36] A second Serbian Orthodox bishopric was in Dabar "with the church of St. Nikola in Polimlje," between Priboj and Prijepolje, at the site where today the monastery of Banja is located. When Polimlje and Podrinje (the Lim and Drina region) were incorporated into Bosnia in 1376, this bishopric of Dabar became Bosnian.

Near Prijepolje on the River Lim, Stjepan Tvrtko I was crowned king of Bosnia and Serbia by the metropolitan of Mileševo in 1377. The establishment of this bishopric is shrouded in darkness.[37]

The Serbian Orthodox church, incessantly at odds with the Catholic church and feuding with the Patarins, could not develop during the period of national independence.

The Patarin Church

The "Bosnian church," as the Patarins preferred to call themselves, was of the three reigning confessions the one with the greatest influence on and significance for the spiritual and political life of Bosnia during its period of national independence.[38]

The Patarins originated in Bulgaria. Toward the end of the tenth century they spread to Serbia but could not settle down, owing to the power of the Orthodox Nemanjić family. They then migrated into Bosnia. There, despite all the opposition to them from without and turmoil within, the Patarin movement struck deep roots, maintained its ground and flourished, and for a long time to come put its mark on the land and the people.

Since the Catholic missionaries were especially zealous in their destruction of Patarin writings, and since the Turkish invasion and the ensuing long drawn-out wars obliterated all traces of culture that were not of Slavic origin, the elements of Patarin belief have only been possible to reconstruct on the basis of its opponents' written refutations. According to these, Patarin doctrine may be described as follows:

> They believe above all else that there are two Gods and that the greater created everything spiritual and invisible and the lesser, meaning Lucifer, everything material and visible. They deny the

human nature of Christ and say that Christ had an unreal and ethereal body. They say that Holy Mary was an angel and not a human being. They also say that Christ did not really suffer and die, neither did he truly arise from the dead, nor ascend to heaven in the flesh.

Except for the Psalms they reject the Old Testament. All the fathers of the Old Testament, the Patriarchs and the Prophets, are considered damned, as is everyone who existed before Christ. They also condemn John the Baptist, saying he is cursed. And the Law of Moses was given by the devil, the devil having revealed himself to Moses in the cloud of fire.

According to them, the Roman church is an abode of idols, and the followers of this church worship idols.

They are the Church of Christ and the descendents of the Apostles. Among them they had one who stated he was the vicar of Christ and St. Peter's successor.

They reject baptism with water and say that no purification from sins is achieved by it. They also say that children cannot be blessed before reaching maturity.

They also deny the resurrection of the body, saying we shall not rise bodily from the dead.

They reject the sacrament of the body of Christ (Holy Communion), as well as confirmation and extreme unction. They also reject the sacrament of matrimony and say that in marriage no one can be saved. In addition they say that the tree of life is a woman, from which Adam ate while recognizing it as such, and for this reason he was expelled from paradise. They also condemn the sacrament of penance, saying that every person who sins must be baptised again. And all sins, they say, are mortal sins and cannot be expiated. They teach that purgatory does not exist. Lucifer went to heaven and stirred up God's angels so that they came down to the earth, and Lucifer enclosed them in human bodies. Likewise they say that people's souls are demons which were cast out from heaven and which, when they have atoned for their sins in one or more bodies, return to heaven.

They also condemn the material church, paintings and icons, especially the holy cross. They forbid too the giving of alms, asserting that almsgiving is no merit. They also deny the giving of oaths: one must swear neither an honest nor a false oath.

Again, they condemn spiritual jurisdiction and punishments, psychological as well as physical, so that it is therefore not permitted to administer capital punishment or banish anyone. The killing of animals is also a mortal sin. All foods made of meat are condemned, and everything derived from meat. Everybody is cursed, they say, who partakes of meat or cheese or eggs or similar products.[39]

It is quite clear that the polemics of these antagonists were bent on making the heresy appear absurd and dangerous, hence their writings in opposition were one-sided and often inconsistent. Various authors endow the Patarins with attributes and vices that frequently stand in open contradiction to each other. For instance, they are reproached by some for "loathing manual labor" while being condemned by others for working even at Easter.[40]

In their pronounced dualist interpretation the Patarins are closely related to the Gnostic sect of the Manicheans, likewise the Paulicians. They appeared in Bulgaria in the tenth century at a time when a great number of Paulicians and Massalians, colonizing in the environs of Plovdiv (Philippopolis), had settled there after having been expelled from Asia Minor by the Byzantine government. Judging by their conspicuously anticlerical spirit and their reformist tendencies—the hallmark of Patarins—this sect was a link in the chain of all such movements that proliferated in the course of the twelfth century in northern Italy and southern France (Boni homines, Patarins, Cathars, Albigenses, Tisserands, etc.).

It goes without saying that to maintain themselves and spread throughout Bosnia, Patarins had to adjust doctrinally to the conditions of life as they existed and to the social arrangements without which no state can be imagined. For this purpose all the faithful were divided into two groups. The smaller one, termed "perfected" (*perfecti, electi*), adhered strictly to the rules and regulations of their religion and thus represented a sort of ecclesiastical elite. The second group, comprising the majority of the faithful, were the ordinary believers (*credentes*).

They could marry, acquire property and dispose of it, eat as they saw fit, engage in war, and so on. They had only to confess their sins publicly and to accept the obligation to join the "perfected," at least at the point of death. That explains why kings and members of the nobility, who lived entirely in the style of Western aristocrats, could practice this religion.

The basic rules of the Patarins listed above meant that their church organization was a very simple one. At the head of the church stood the *djed* (senior, *ancianus*); below him were the *strojnici* (regulators, teachers, *magistri*). In Bosnia there were twelve of these. The *gost* and the *starac* ("guest" and "elder") had special functions. The first was as a rule successor to the *djed*. There was no hierarchy in the Christian church sense. Their ritual was very simple as well, in keeping with these principles. The service consisted of the Lord's Prayer, reading from the Scriptures, public confession, admission of new believers, and the ordination of *strojnici*. Churches were plain houses: no decoration, no embellishment, no pictures or statues—like the sign of the cross, these were prohibited—and neither bells, which they characterized as "demon trumpets," nor holy water, which they "loathed like poison."

The main reason that Patarins struck deep roots in Bosnia and spread rapidly was above all because the people of that time were too little conversant with the Christian faith. Without a doubt there were elements in the Patarin belief itself that exerted a compelling power over the young Slavic race—a people still torn between "heathen concepts with dualistic coloring" and unclear Christian dogmas. But the whole phenomenon is so enveloped in darkness that one can hardly attach to it a wide-ranging reform significance nor dare engage in the kind of risky analogies we encounter here and there in the literature.[41]

What is most certain and, for us, most important is the fact that Patarins knew how to adjust to Bosnian conditions; the fact that their faith thus became the people's faith; and the fact that insofar as there did exist a criterion by which the country's internal organization could be judged or a palladium in Bosnia's struggle against foreign intervention, this faith carried weight. In their unequal, bitter fight with Catholicism, the Patarins had begun to erect that wall of stone between Bosnia and the Western world which in the course of time was to be enlarged still more by Islam and raised to such mighty heights that even today, although long since crumbled and fallen to pieces, it still produces the effect of a dark, demarcating line that one dare not step over without effort and danger. To conclude: the Patarins, with their stiff-necked refusal to be subjugated to the West, inevitably brought the country under the yoke of the East. Catholic propaganda, for its part employing the means we have mentioned earlier, contributed in full measure to this fateful end.

Development of Spiritual and Political Preconditions for the Turkish Conquest

Driven by the pressures of these involved, abnormal religious and political conditions, Bosnia little by little ripened toward its fall; it became "entangled in the chains of the Turkish sultans," as Klaić put it, "well before the onset of the fatal catastrophe of 1463."[42]

The delegates from Ragusa, attending the congress to elect the king in Visoko in 1404 and clearly observing the general fragmentation and decline, were quite right when they reported to their council that "not since the Deluge has the dizzy, dazed world been in such a mess."[43] Similarly in 1416 the people of Ragusa could write to the queen of Hungary that "Bosnam destructam esse penitus et barones ipsos intra se exterminium maximum preparare." [Bosnia is being torn apart from within and its barons are themselves contriving their own maximum eviction.][44] There was no order in the country, no obedience, only arbitrary power, plunder and looting.[45] In such an unhealthy situation it seemed entirely reasonable to proceed as did the Byzantines or the princes of Serbia: to call on the Turks for help, one side against the other, whenever momentary personal or party interests demanded it, "following the custom of the time."

The Frenchman Bertrandon de la Broquière, who traveled in Turkey and in 1432 was granted an audience by the sultan, brings into his description of the court ceremony in Adrianople the following interesting note: "Once all were seated, a certain gentleman from the kingdom of Bosnia was given permission to enter. He had come for the purpose of turning his country over to the sultan. They showed him to a place on the divan in the row of pashas and he asked the sultan for help against the Bosnian king, claiming that this kingdom belonged to him."[46]

Now, we have it on quite reliable authority that bargaining with the Turks had long been prevalent, perhaps even from the moment they had first appeared on the Bosnian border, and that on this point all transgressed in equal measure, kings, nobles, and the common people alike. Even in the year 1398, in a letter sent to the inhabitants of Trau [Trogir], the Hungarian king Sigismund complained of the most powerful of the Bosnian magnates, Hrvoje Vukčić, that "se ipsum in coetum infidelium crucis Christi, Turcorum videlicet, connumerare et coadunare" [that "he reckons himself among their number, he counts himself as one with those unfaithful to the Cross of Christ, namely, the Turks"].[47] In like manner, a few years later this same Hrvoje Vukčić accused King Ostoja of having long been in league with the Turks (. . . "iamdiu se adhaeserit Turchis et rebellibus Bosnensibus") [. . . by now he will have been clinging to the Turks and rebellious Bosnians for a long time].[48] It seems that conniving with the Turks was a common vice in which almost everyone indulged when convenient, only to use it afterwards as an argument to defame the opposition.

We cannot truly judge the motivation of such dealings on the part of the nobles without keeping in sight the moral standards of the time, without visualizing the political perspectives present in the minds of these nobles.[49] Among the nobility—notwithstanding the many customs and advances they had adopted—a sense of belonging to the great community of Western Christendom was poorly developed. Far more did they regard their own habit of leaning now toward the intruders from the East, now toward the Christian West, as only a matter of tactics in the struggle for worldly property and spiritual independence.

As we mentioned elsewhere Catholicism, and with it Western culture, came to Bosnia mainly through Hungarian arms. This meant the political supremacy of a foreign, alien power whose support could be used to advantage in case of momentary need but against whom, should the opportunity arise, one could always call upon another foreign power. We know that the Serbian despot Đurađ Branković, given a choice between the sultan, who guaranteed him religious freedom, and the Hungarian regent Hunyadi, who proposed his converting to Catholicism, preferred to affiliate with the former rather than with the Christian prince.[50] For Bosnia this must have been all the more critical a moment because what was at issue was the Patarin community of belief. And that community—to go no further than its own fundamental doctrinal principles—was a sect that, according to Rački, had not originated in the church, as by branching off from it, but must rather be considered a religious community "rooted in dualism and heathen theosophy, which means that it was outside Christianity and recognized Christian dogmas only insofar as the latter did not openly conflict with dualistic principles."[51]

However, apart from spiritual and political preconditions there were also socioeconomic factors that opened the way into Bosnia for the Turks. In the letter mentioned above, sent by the last Bosnian king Stjepan Tomašević to Pope Pius II in which he makes an urgent plea for help, there is also the following passage: "The Turks have built several fortresses in my kingdom and are very kind to the country folk. *They promise freedom to every peasant who converts to Islam.* The simple peasant mind cannot see through such shrewd cunning and believes that this freedom will last forever."[52]

It is also on record that the people of Ragusa, wrangling with Stjepan Vukčić, duke of St. Sava (1451–53), accused him among other things of being the first to bring Turks into the country when he called on Barah-Paša and 1,500 Turks for help in suppressing a rebellion by his peasants.[53]

And so we see that the Turks knew how to turn discord of this sort to their own advantage, pressing on into the country now as supporters of the nobility, now as protectors of the peasantry. It must not be forgotten that they brought to the land they were penetrating—a land politically and socially splintered, a land in anarchy—the opposing virtues of unity, absolute administrative centralization, iron discipline, and blind obedience. Nor should it be forgotten that they could counter Bosnia's crippling religious quarrels with a faith, firm as a rock, of their own. Attaining to the quality of fanaticism, it was a faith that conferred upon the Turks their joy of attack and their staying power.[54]

The prescription for disaster was well in hand. Slowly the year of general ruin and inglorious decline, the year 1463, drew nearer.

2 The Spread of Islam as a Direct Effect of Turkish Rule

Partial Conversion to Islam

A snapshot view of spiritual and religious life in the Kingdom of Bosnia was the aim of the previous chapter, together with the political circumstances in which it was closely embedded. Such questions, however, as to whether there was any culture in Bosnia at all, or what its nature might be, or what level it had reached before the Turks suppressed and destroyed it, are not in themselves of paramount importance when we weigh the impact of Turkish hegemony on the country's spiritual life. What is decisive is the fact that at the most critical juncture in its spiritual development, with its spiritual powers in ferment, Bosnia was conquered by an Asiatic military people whose social institutions and customs spelled the negation of any and all Christian culture and whose religion—begotten under other skies and social circumstances and quite incapable of adaptation—shackled the life of the spirit and the mind in Bosnia, disfiguring it and molding it into an exceptional case [*Ausnahmeerscheinung*].[1]

Like Serbia, Bosnia too on the eve of invasion by the Turks "was making the transition that constitutes one of the most crucial moments in the life of every nation, when out of dark, patriarchal and parochial beginnings it passes on to a stage shaped by spiritual awareness corresponding to the general development of the human race and to the legitimized ordering of affairs."[2]

The situation in Bosnia was all the more awkward on account of the frightful religious struggle that was raging within the country. As mentioned, this struggle had reached a critical point just before the invasion when some resolution was unavoidable, whatever the direction taken. Bosnia might have turned entirely to the Catholic West and participated to the fullest in its spiritual life. (The fact that two of the last Bosnian kings openly leaned toward Catholicism, followed by a respectable number of the nobility, makes this the most likely possibility.) Or on the other hand, less plausible, a kind of minor scale Slavic Reformation in Bosnia's spiritual life would have been brought about by a victory of the Patarins.[3]

At the decisive moment this far-reaching process was abruptly broken by the sudden intrusion of a conquering people foreign in faith, spirit, and race. The confusion was compounded when the upper, better-off part of the population, in order to save its possessions, adopted the religion of these intruders. So it came about that down the middle of the South Slavic lands a line was etched, a line generally following the Danube, Sava, and Una rivers and the Dinaric Alps if we disregard strong fluctuations. This dividing wall split in two the Serbo-Croatian racial and linguistic complex and its shadow, where four centuries of ghastly history were played out, was to lie heavy on the landscape to either side into the far distant future.

Therein we see the whole meaning of Turkish rule and Turkish influence on Bosnia's spiritual life.

By right of geographic position Bosnia should have linked the lands along the Danube with the Adriatic Sea, two peripheries of the Serbo-Croatian element and two different zones of European culture. Having fallen to Islam, it was in no position to fulfill this, its natural role, and to take part in the cultural development of Christian Europe, to which ethnographically and geographically it belonged. What is more, thanks to the domestic Islamized element Bosnia even became a mighty bulwark against the Christian West. And in that unnatural posture it was to stay for the entire duration of Turkish rule.

Conversion by the Nobility

How the process of Islamization, so important for spiritual development, actually proceeded cannot be traced with certainty nor established in detail. As the more recent historians interpret it, the Turks, in the first decades of their rule, went to great pains to adapt themselves to local cultural conditions, leaving assimilation to the workings of time.[4] That is not hard to grasp. Such behavior, however, on the part of the Turks should not be ascribed to some preconceived plan nor understood as the outcome of a tolerance nowhere to be found in later days. The fact that during early Turkish times in Bosnia, and especially in Hercegovina, we still run across Christian landowners and administrative officials means no more than that conversion was still proceeding *slowly* and *gradually*. It must not be overlooked that all Bosnia became a battleground after the fall of the kingdom. In the neighborhood of Jajce, Hungarian armies were met in battle repeatedly for the next sixty years. Quite naturally it follows that the Turks could not act as absolute masters on this territory, insecure and disputed as it was. To some extent they had to make allowances for at least the more respected and prosperous elements in the population.

After the fall of Jajce in 1528, Islamization went ahead ruthlessly and quickly and was all over by the end of the sixteenth century. Truhelka's assertion that there are no examples or proof of enforced conversion is completely wrong.[5] The whole situation created by the Turkish invasion, a complex of interrelated psychic and material facts, presented the Bosnian nobility and all the landowning class with the following dilemma: either keep land and power in their own hands and thereby gain access to all the dignities of the new empire, or lose everything and become landless *rayah* without rights.[6] Whoever wished to retain his property for good along with the political ascendancy and privileges vested in it had finally to convert to Islam.[7]

Such a dilemma was tantamount to forced conversion. To get a clear grasp of this we have to keep in the forefront of our attention how tightly the Bosnian nobility clung to its land and property [*Grund und Boden*].[8] In a country like Bosnia, where even at the best of times only a small percentage of the soil has been arable, land has been of particularly high value. This value was increased still more by the legal and social arrangements on which ownership was based. Landed property was received from the king as "noble inheritance" (*plemenita baština*) in exchange for extraordinary services and was to be held in undisputed possession. Such territorial holding was free of compulsory service and tax (*prosta od sveh robot i podanak*) and was granted "in perpetuity" to the one so favored "and to his heirs."[9] Thus landed property became the main source of the family's personal honor and power.

Grave inscriptions dating from that time bear eloquent witness to a deep, elemental attachment to landed property.[10] Formulaic inscriptions laying a curse upon anyone damaging a gravestone or attempting to move it are common. ("Here lie I on my *very own ground* who myself this stone have carved and written thereon. Cursed be he who lays hand to it.")[11] The most sacred and solemn formulas were used to fix ownership and safeguard real estate.[12]

Confronted therefore by the dilemma we have stated, the Bosnian nobleman, ever swayed by atavistic love for and attachment to his freehold, decided in favor of "the Kingdom of this world." In order to save his real estate he accepted the faith of his conquerors and at once set about nailing down that property with its associated rights and privileges all the more tightly and securely using the precepts and formulas of the new religion, the more the old one was denied.

The later history of Bosnia and Bosnian large landed property likewise offers evidence that we make no mistake in lending such weight to this aspect of the conversion: landed property continued henceforth to be the mainspring of all transactions among the Islamized Bosnian noblemen, whether they were enlarging their property or defending it. The nobleman's ideal continued to be personal property on which he could do as he pleased, exactly as it had been his ideal at the time of the kingdom. In any religious and political allegiance he saw only a means of holding onto property. Such property remained the principal aim of all his strivings and struggles.[13]

Even when Turkish rule was at its height, the Bosnian begs who were the mainstay of its power carefully preserved "their old deeds and privileges granted them by the Christian kings(!), so as to be able to produce them should a Christian ruler again reign in Bosnia."[14] And when, in the nineteenth century, the sultans tried to introduce a few reforms that would have jeopardized their property and their power, these Bosnian begs rose up in arms and formally warred against the very sultans whose "pampered children" they were.[15]

In short, whether it was the Ottoman conception of the state or the Kingdom of Bosnia, whether it was Islam or the Patarins, each was seen only as a means of maintaining landed property and the power that came with it.

The following excerpt from a folk song of Mohammedan origin plainly indicates how conversion took its course:

Beg je Rada lijepo poturčio
I sa lijepom Anom oženio,
Darovo mu deset kuća kmeta,
Ne zove se sada Radojica,
Već se zove Pilipović Ibro.

(The beg did a pretty good job of making Rado a Turk
And he *married him off* to pretty Anna too,
Gave him ten households of field hands,
Now no longer is he called Radojica,
Now they call him Ibro Pilipović.)[16]

Those few verses ring with the recurrent leitmotifs of conversion to Islam. But they also imply that the Islamized Bosnians, in some cases at least, stuck to their old Slavic names. The same understanding, only more radically expressed, of the motives and circumstances surrounding conversion is found in works reflecting the national spirit among the Christian part of the population. Njegoš, who can always be counted on for the truest expression of the people's mode of thinking and apprehending, portrays in his terse and plastic manner the process of conversion thus:[17] "Postadoše lafi ratarima, / Isturči se plahi i lakomi." (The lions turned into tillers of the soil, / The cowardly and the covetous turned into Turks.)*

The Franciscan I. F. Jukić characterizes the Bosnian Muslims fully in the spirit of Christian popular perception: "They sprang from the bad Christians who turned Muslim because only thus could they protect their land. . . . The new faith secured to them their property and wealth, freed them of all taxes and assessments, and gave them carte blanche to indulge in any vice, any evil dealing, all for the sake of living as great lords without toil and effort."[18]

The Boy-Tribute

There was another institution brought by the conqueror and imposed by force on the subjugated land, one of great importance for Islamiza-

---

*By "lions" Njegoš meant the Christian fighters who remained loyal to the beliefs of their forefathers.—Author.

tion and hence for Bosnia's spiritual life: the Adžami-Oglan or boy-tribute [*devshirme*].

The well-known traveler Bartholomäus Georgiewitz described this special kind of tax. He based his account on personal experience, having spent a number of years as a prisoner in Turkey. He later depicted the life-style, customs, and habits of the Turks in numerous works, as well as the position of Christians under their rule as follows:[19]

> Apart from the other *tax burdens* which the Christians had to bear under Turkish rule, from time to time their handsomest offspring were seized from them. Separating the children from their parents, the Turks would instruct them in the martial arts. These children, abducted by force, never returned to their parents. Alienated from the Christian religion, little by little they forgot faith, parents, brothers and sisters, and all their blood relatives, so that when they later encountered their parents they no longer even recognized them.

> I can find no right words to picture the pain and sorrow, the weeping and wailing of these parents when their children were torn from their bosoms and out of their grasp by those fiends. To parents who had just barely begun to instruct their children in Christian teaching, the hardest thought was that the evildoers would soon succeed in seducing them away from the religion of their forebears and in turning them into dreadful enemies of the Christian religion and of Christian people.[20]

Every five years special commissioners were sent out from Constantinople known as *telosnici*, from *telos*, the name of this tax. Spreading throughout the state, they traveled from place to place, village to village. Every head of a family had to declare accurately the number of his children and bring them before the commissioner. Concealment was severely punished. There was no rule stating that a given number of children was to be taken from each household; only the total was specified and it was left up to the commissioner to select those that were healthiest and best looking.[21]

Understandably, Christian parents resorted to every imaginable means of saving their children and keeping them by their side.

The most common stratagem was to bribe the commissioner, whom money might induce to choose one child over some other. This also explains why the sultan's court officials eagerly vied for the assignment.[22] Parents who could not bribe their way to their goal because they were too poor would attempt to hide their child. And all too often they resorted to crippling it or otherwise so disfiguring the child that they could be quite sure of keeping it in their own custody. Since it was not allowed to take young married men, often it happened that children were married off as early as eleven or twelve years of age.[23]

The Venetian ambassador A. Contarini at the beginning of the seventeenth century journeyed through the South Slavic lands, and he describes a rescue method that was especially characteristic. There were Christian parents, he says, who to forestall having to hand over their children to the janissaries paid their fellow countrymen who had already converted to Islam money (*"qualche recognitione"*) to substitute their own offspring. It was something these converts were only too happy to do in hopes that their own children might thus achieve high honors in Constantinople.[24]

The impact of this system and of the way it was executed hardly needs pointing out. It would be superfluous to dwell on how it affected the spiritual life of the conquered land. As early as three years after the collapse of the Bosnian kingdom, in 1467, the first *telosnik* arrived to gather up "the Christian lads." From then until the seventeenth century Bosnia was ever haunted by the commissioners of the Porte in pursuit of this objective.[25] The abducted children soon forgot, as we said, their paternal hearth and faith and turned into fanatic "Turks." Descendants of roughhewn, healthy mountain folk, with their inborn intelligence and ability, they won honor and respect much more readily than did the lazy, vice-ridden Turks. The echo of their wealth and renown could be heard all the way back to Bosnia, and it had a seductive effect upon their countrymen and relations. "This won for Islam far more proselytes than the most zealous of preachers or clerics ever could do."[26]

We might well understand that this institution sowed confusion in the land, split families asunder, and left the people as a whole disunited.[27]

3 The Social and Administrative Institutions of Islam, as Embodied in Turkish Sovereignty, and Their Impact on the Life of the Non-Muslim Population

Islamic Views of Non-Muslims in Bosnia

The Kanun-i-Rayah

The single criterion of life in the countries conquered by the Turks was Islam, be it personal, social, material, or spiritual life. The life of the mind and spirit developed under conditions imposed by Islam, not only for those who embraced it but for all Turkish subjects irrespective of faith. For that part of Bosnia's population that would not accept Islam, those conditions were spelled out in part by the *Kanun-i-Rayah* (*rayah* code of law). This consists of a set of regulations prescribed by the second caliph, Omar al-Chatab, for Christians and Jews in conquered Damascus (635 A.D.). Somewhat altered in form and moderated in tone, the same regulations became valid for all the rest of the provinces of the Turkish empire.*

The collection reads as follows:

1. Christians and Jews in subjugated lands are not to erect any monasteries, churches or hermitages.
2. They are not to repair their churches.
3. Those who live in the vicinity of Muslims may repair their houses only under urgent necessity.
4. They are to enlarge the gates of their monasteries and churches for the benefit of passing travelers.
5. They are to offer three full days of hospitality to all strangers.

---

*See Joseph Hammer-Purgstall, *Des Osmanischen Reichs Staatsverfassung und Staatsverwaltung* (Vienna, 1815), I: 183–86.

6. They are not to harbor spies, and if they recognize such they shall turn them over to the Muslims.
7. Their children are not to be taught the Koran.
8. They are not to administer justice among themselves.
9. They are not to hinder any of their number from becoming a Muslim.
10. They shall behave deferentially toward Muslims, rise when they enter, and vacate the place of honor without grumbling.
11. They are not to wear the same clothes and shoes as Muslims.
12. They are not to learn scholarly Arabic (the written language).
13. They are not to mount any saddled horse nor carry a saber or other weapon, either within doors or outside.
14. They are not to sell wine nor let their hair grow.
15. They are not to engrave their names in signet rings.
16. They are not to wear wide sashes.
17. They are not to wear the cross nor carry their holy writings openly outside their homes.
18. Indoors, they must not ring loudly, only softly.
19. Indoors, they may sing only with muted voices.
20. They may pray for their dead only in silence.
21. Muslims may till the soil and sow in Christian cemeteries when they are no longer used for funerals.
22. Christians and Jews are not to keep slaves.
23. They are not to purchase Muslim prisoners nor look into the houses of Muslims.
24. If a Christian or Jew is mistreated by a Muslim, the latter shall pay the penalty fixed thereon.

Doubtless not every one of these disabilities was applied literally and precisely in practice. It is also quite certain that Christians and Jews, as we shall see later in more detail, were able to circumvent or thwart many an item of the *Kanun,* either through bribery or cunning. Besides, it was of no great importance to the Turks themselves whether the *rayah* observed some of the smaller, less meaningful prescriptions.[1]

Neglect of Non-Muslims

We have, though, at our disposal a wealth of irrefutable evidence that the main points of the *Kanun,* just those that cut the deepest into the moral and economic life of Christians, remained in full force right up to the end of Turkish rule and as long as the Turks had the power to apply them. On the basis of the sources at hand we shall try to show briefly how far individual points of the *Kanun* were applied in Bosnia, and with what consequences. Likewise we shall depict the living conditions forced by Turkish rule on nonbelievers, conditions that, directly or indirectly, must have had an impact on the spiritual life of the Bosnian *rayah*.

Even if we proceed from Islam's conceptual foundation before taking up the way it was put into practice, it was inevitable that the *rayah* decline to a status that was economically inferior and dependent.[2] In addition to which it should be noted that during the entire first half of Turkish hegemony Bosnia was either a battlefield or at minimum a staging ground for troops to collect and sally out on massive, profitable campaigns of conquest into Hungary. Under such conditions it is easy to see how the *rayah* must have made significant sacrifices to the demands of war and military caprice, over and above the usual heavy taxes in kind and conscript labor.[3] Christians, therefore, began to abandon their houses and plots of land situated in level country and along the roads and to retreat back into the mountains. And as they did so, moving ever higher into inaccessible regions, Muslims took over their former sites.[4] Thus there came about the characteristic population distribution that is to be seen in Bosnia to this very day.[5]

The growing physical isolation of a people who were scattered enough as it was and their increasing remoteness from public roads and centers of culture could not have remained without consequence for the cultural and moral development of any Christian person.[6] Those Christians, however, who did live in the towns conducting business and trade found the existing laws of the Islamic system to be an outright impediment to any mercantile advance and even to provide inadequate protection for their inventory of stock. Islam, from the very outset, excluded such activities as making wine, breeding pigs, and selling pork products from commercial production and trade.[7] But additionally Bosnian Christians were forbidden to be sadlers, tanners, or candlemakers or to trade in honey, butter, and certain other items.[8] Countrywide, the only legal market day was Sunday. Christians were thus deliberately faced with the choice between ignoring the precepts of their religion, keeping their shops open and working on Sundays, or alternatively, forgoing participation in the market and suffering material loss thereby. Even in 1850, in Jukić's "Wishes and Entreaties" [*Želje i molbe*] we find him beseeching "his Imperial grace" to put an end to the regulation that Sunday be market day.[9]

The taxes paid by Christians were not only disproportionately higher than those paid by Muslims, but also the way they were collected was marked by neither justice nor dignity. The levy of the poll tax (*arač*), especially, was "personally degrading." This tax was paid by every non-Muslim male who had passed his fourteenth year, at the rate of a ducat per annum. But since Turkey had never known birth registers (*matriken*), the functionary whose job it was to exact the tax measured the head and neck of each boy with a piece of string and judged from that whether a person had arrived at taxable age or not.[10] Starting as an abuse that soon turned into ingrained habit, then finally established custom, by the last century of Turkish rule every boy without distinction as to age found himself summoned to pay the head tax. And it would seem this was not the only abuse.[11]

Generally speaking, social inequality and moral backwardness went hand in hand with economic subordination.

Until the middle of the nineteenth century the Turkish authorities insisted on strict adherence to the stipulations contained in points 13, 14, and 16 of the *Kanun*. In the year 1794 Hussamudin-Paša passed a special ordinance exactly prescribing not only the color but also the kind of clothing the Bosnian *rayah* had to wear.[12] A church proclamation from this period located in the archives of the Serbian Orthodox church in Sarajevo proves that the Turkish authorities were ever intent on the strictest observance of these ordinances. In it the church administration, on orders from the vizier, demanded that the faithful hold rigorously to the 1794 dress code.[13]

The account books of the Jewish community in Sarajevo known as the *Pinakes* and dating from this period reveal that the Spanish Jews domiciled in Bosnia from the mid-sixteenth century were subject to the same regulations as the Christians, displayed the selfsame inclination to dress like the ruling classes, and were penalized as a result. As a rule such penalties were converted to monetary fines or bribes.[14]

Barbers were not allowed to shave Christians with the same razors used for Muslims. Christians even in bathhouses had to have specially marked aprons and towels so as to make it impossible to confuse their laundry with that designated for Muslims.[15] When encountering a Muslim a Christian had to jump down from his horse, step to the side of the road, and wait for the former to pass by; only then could he remount and continue on his own way. This obligation was set aside in about 1850 after Omer-Paša overpowered the Muslim oligarchy in Bosnia.[16] Rośkiewicz, however, who traveled in Bosnia in 1863, confirmed that in some areas the custom, which he spoke of as "downright degrading," still survived.[17]

Obstacles to Church Life

To build a new church of any Christian confession whatever was out of the question. To restore existing ones as well as monasteries was sanctioned only with a firman from the sultan. Moreover, as we shall see, restoration was fraught with enormous costs, complications, and not infrequently, dangers. An imperial firman dating to 1641 and approving repairs to the church and the Franciscan monastery at Fojnica plainly shows how the Bosnian *rayah* kept up their churches. We can see as well something of the conditions under which the building trades generally could develop in that era:

> The monks from the Fojnica monastery having appeared in court to complain that their church and their monastery are dilapidated to the point of collapse and in need of repair; and they having expressed the wish that permission be granted them to bring both structures back to their former state; now therefore, assuming that the aforesaid declaration rests on the truth and that the church in question was erected *before and not after the conquest of Bosnia,* I hereby command with the appropriate imperial firman that no obstacle be placed in the way of restoration, on condition that the repairs are to be undertaken only in those places that absolutely require it and *only with planks,* and let them take strict care that the church not be enlarged in any of its dimensions and that in the course of the repair work no *stone or earth* be employed.[18]

The intent of this arrangement was plain as a pikestaff: to hamper the repair of existing monasteries and churches and to forbid the construction of new ones in the expectation that in time they would all disappear.

In 1762, the roofs of the three existing monasteries and their churches having rotted out, the Franciscans dispatched two of their brethren to Constantinople to ask the sultan's permission to put on new roofs. The provincial of the order, Fra Marijan Bogdanović, issued a circular letter on this occasion in which he charged that God be prayed to daily "to soften and inspire the heart of the sultan." In the meantime, while the envoys were still tarrying in Constantinople, the permission they sought was obtained through bribery from the vizier (governor), Mehmed-Paša.[19]

In 1765 the monastery in Kreševo burned down and the Franciscans, forced to live in little huts, the following year sent two deputations to Constantinople seeking approval to rebuild. Both returned with empty hands. Not until the year after that, 1767, did the order succeed in its efforts to reconstruct the monastery, after having bribed the entire Bosnian administrative cadre, from vizier down to kadi [judge]. Bills of account for this affair of the Kreševo monastery show that labor and material cost the Franciscans 3,313 groš, while for bribing the Turkish authorities and "a few domestic Muslims" they distributed the sum of 8,973 groš. The outlay for bribery and building license more than twice exceeded the costs of actual construction work.[20]

The chronicles and protocols of the other monasteries paint a similar picture of the position of Christians in this respect. When in the year 1730 the monastery in Sutjeska was repaired with the approval of Vizier Ahmed-Paša, who was "not entirely against Catholics," certain domestic Muslims denounced the Franciscans "for having hidden some cannon in the walls." Upon hearing this, the vizier sent a commission crowded with members under instructions to verify the truth of the claim on the spot. "They sat around here in the church for about fifteen days but we couldn't straighten the matter out with them." In the end the vizier was paid off with 500 groš, the rest of the Turks with 200 groš, and so the affair was settled.[21]

Monasteries and rectories alike mirrored existing conditions in their style of construction. Owing to lack of security and frequent attacks, cloisters were situated far from roads, as a rule in the middle of the mountains or in gorges. Fra Paolo de Rovigno, who made a tour of inspection [*visitator*] in the year 1640 of the Bosnian monasteries, said of the one at Tuzla that it "looked more like some prison den than a human habitation: candles had to be kept burning in broad daylight."[22] As late as the eighties of the last century, Hoernes could still verify the evidence and effects of Turkish rule in the building style of Christian rectories.[23] The fact that the same conditions obtained for the *rayah* of the other religious confessions is illustrated by this example: In the year 1794 the Jews of Sarajevo won permission through an imperial firman to rebuild their synagogue, which had recently burned down. It hardly need be said that the usual stipulations applied. "No more than any of the other confessions are they allowed to enlarge such a structure by so much as a jot or a tittle in the process of reerecting it."[24] And to the imperial firman were attached the usual formalities—permission of the vizier, permission of the kadi, two separate commissions, and so on. All this took more than two years and cost a tidy sum.[25]

It was also obligatory in Bosnia to receive and accommodate traveling Muslims. At minimum this can be stated categorically for Catholic and Serbian Orthodox monasteries. As early as 1515 we find the guardian of the monastery in Fojnica asking the Turkish authorities for permission to build a *musafirhana,* or hostel, next to his monastery "where Muslims coming to Fojnica can be lodged and fed gratis without their having to enter the monastery itself, as has been the custom heretofore."[26] All the way up into the nineteenth century this right was claimed by the Turks. In 1849 the monks of the Serbian Orthodox monastery Duži reported to the patriarch in Constantinople that they did not have enough bread "because their guests—*musafiri*—were a heavy burden."[27] Lacking written evidence, it is more difficult to determine the degree to which the Turks made use of this prerogative of theirs with respect to private dwellings. The proverb "You don't get a winter without a wind or take in a troublemaker without a Turk" indicates that the right was used and indeed often abused. (*Nema zime bez vjetra, ni zla gosta bez Turčina.*)

About point 17 of the *Kanun-i-Rayah:* In the chronicle of the Franciscan monastery in Kreševo to which we have referred, monetary penalties are often mentioned which the Franciscans had to pay on grounds that at somebody's funeral they had worn their crosses publicly.[28]

Bells—the loudest and most arresting symbols of Christianity—have always riveted the attention of Turks. Wherever their invasions would go, down came the bells, to be destroyed or melted into cannon.[29] Until the second half of the nineteenth century "nobody in Bosnia could even think of bells or bell towers."[30] Only in 1860 did the Sarajevo priest Fra Grgo Martić manage to get permission from Topal Osman-Paša to hang a bell at the church in Kreševo.[31] Permission was granted, though, only on condition that "at first the bell be rung softly to let the Turks get accustomed to it little by little." And still the Muslims of Kreševo were complaining, even in 1875, to Sarajevo that "the Turkish ear and ringing bells cannot coexist in the same place at the same time"; and Muslim women would beat on their copper pots to drown out the noise.[32] In 1870 the governor granted permission to Fra Grgo Martić to hang the first bell in the Catholic church of Sarajevo. That concession was preceded, however, by prolonged negotiations between the vizier and the Muslim clergy over the issue of "whether a Muslim can live in a place where bells ring without its being counted a sin." Their disputes were so vehement and went to such lengths that one fanatic cleric "hit his opponent over the head with the holy book." In the end the vizier managed to break the opposition of the fanatics. So at Easter in the year 1871 the first bell was hung with great ceremony in the presence of foreign consuls.[33] One year later, on 30 April 1872, the new Serbian Orthodox church also got a bell. But since the native-born Muslims had threatened to riot, the military had to be called in to ensure that the ceremony might proceed undisturbed.[34]

In the year 1801 the Franciscans contrived to import an organ from Austria for their monastery in Fojnica. After overcoming all problems in transporting and installing the organ, when it was ready to be played the town's Muslim populace rose up in revolt, denouncing the Franciscans to the vizier and claiming that "they have acquired too noisy a music-making instrument, one which will disturb the domestic peace and the saying of prayers." Only through a sizable bribe was permission obtained to play the instrument, together with a prohibition against Muslims walking into the church "to stare at this wonderwork."[35]

That the disability was not simply imposed on church ceremonies is apparent from the proclamation mentioned above, issued by the Serbian Orthodox church in Sarajevo: "and they (i.e., the *rayah*) may not sing during said outings, nor in their houses, nor in other places."[36] The saying "Don't sing too loud, this village is Turk" testifies eloquently to the fact that that item of the *Kanun* was applied outside church life as well as within.

Bosnian Backwardness

Quite apart from these impediments, which applied only to the *rayah*, general conditions were extremely unfavorable for cultural development. Roads, which even until very recent times had been of no concern at all to the Turkish administration, were few in number and extremely primitive. Conveyance of merchandise was managed by the typical *kiridžije* [carters], who traveled only during daylight hours in caravans of one to two hundred horses. Transportation was expensive, troublesome, and uncertain. All travelers, even those in the nineteenth century, depict means of transport and Bosnian road conditions in the darkest of colors.[37] Local writers and chronicles only fill in this general picture.[38]

It was the energetic Topal Osman-Paša who began building the two main roads through Bosnia toward the end of Turkish rule in 1860, the one from Mostar to Sarajevo and the other from Sarajevo to Brod. Construction of the short stretch between Mostar and Sarajevo took eleven years. The state spent an enormous sum (250,000 Gulden) and in addition the population—Christians, naturally—"from all Hercegovina and half Bosnia" had to work on the project without pay, in the course of which many sickened and died.[39] Despite it all only the Austrian administration after 1878 could finish this road. Construction of the second, very important, road could not progress at all because the Bosnian Muslims threatened a riot and accused Osman-Paša of building it with the object of "bringing the Germans to Bosnia."[40]

Mail service mirrored the hopeless condition of the public road system. Only in 1844 did Ćamil-Paša, known as "Muhendis" ("the Engineer"), introduce a regular weekly postal connection via mounted messengers between Constantinople and Travnik.[41] Letters addressed in a foreign language were never delivered, postal clerks being unable to read anything but Turkish. Such letters were simply put into a basket at the post office and anyone interested could go and collect the correspondence meant for him.[42] The postal administration also kept horses for travelers, but they were so expensive to use that only the very rich, generally foreigners, could afford this means of transport. Foreign consulates maintained their own postal connections with border towns. These conditions were prevalent up to the last year of Turkish rule. A hindrance to traffic inside the country, an obstacle likewise to cultural communication with the outside, they contributed to the isolation of individual areas and to the general neglect of the country as a whole.[43] All these things jointly conspired to block the path of any technical advance making its way into Bosnia, even the most common of European civilization's achievements. And this at a time when such achievements had long been exercising their beneficial effect on the life of the mind and spirit in those South Slavic countries that lay outside the Ottoman Empire.

In 1493 the first Serbian printing press was founded in Obod, near Cetinje. Soon thereafter, about the year 1520, a second press "for soul-saving books" was established in Goražde, on Bosnian territory. This too, like the one in Mileševo built in 1544, lasted only a short time. By the second half of the sixteenth century not a trace remained of any of these printing presses. While in the rest of Europe the art of printing was visibly spreading and thriving, Bosnia was turning back to the Middle Ages in this regard as well, "but without the political independence of the Middle Ages."[44] The Catholic clergy had whatever was indispensable printed outside the country, mostly in Italy. The effect on Bosnian literature was negative, both spiritually and materially. The Serbian Orthodox clergy, on the other hand, having no connections or support abroad, went back to copying out books *by hand* and had to resort to this production method well into the eighteenth century. In his "Wishes and Entreaties of Bosnian and Hercegovinian Christians," referred to above, Jukić requests in item 14 that "a printing shop for Christians be set up at state expense."[45] In the end those "wishes" remained unfulfilled, only bringing banishment to their author and costing him his life. The urgent need, however, for a press came to be felt more and more keenly. So in 1853 the Franciscans—this time very cautiously—approached Mehmed Huršid-Paša to beg that "a small print shop be allowed to open in Sarajevo and that it be put in

sisted of two parts: an examination in the candidate's major field of study, in this case Slavic philology (*Hauptrigorosum*), and an examination on the history of Austria (*Nebenrigorosum*), Andrić's minor area. On 3 June 1924 Andrić passed his *Hauptrigorosum* with the grade of "excellent," the highest possible mark, from the three-member examining committee. Nine days later he passed the *Nebenrigorosum* with the same mark. One day after his final examination, 13 June 1924, he was awarded the degree of Doctor of Philosophy from the University of Graz. Soon thereafter he requested his former employer, the Royal Yugoslav Ministry for Foreign Affairs in Belgrade, that he be reinstated into the diplomatic service and be given a position approximately reflecting his newly acquired academic status. In September 1924, now Dr. Andrić, he was indeed made once more a vice-consul in his former place of service, the Royal Yugoslav Consulate in Graz.

Undoubtedly the most important part of Andrić's doctoral studies is his dissertation. Composed in a relatively short period of time, it is an important document in this writer's rich and varied literary inheritance. It is the only scholarly document in the oeuvre of Ivo Andrić, a famous author. Although it was found to have sufficient merit to meet the standards of scholarly publications and was, indeed, recommended by the official readers for publication, Andrić never pursued this recommendation. What were the possible reasons? A closer look at both the terms of the readers' recommendation and the merits and shortcomings of Andrić's thesis may suggest some answers.

In their report Schmid and Kaindl found the subject of Andrić's dissertation both interesting and new. It was the first detailed and amply supported study, they thought, of the impact of four and more centuries of Turkish rule on Bosnia's spiritual and literary life. The account books kept by the Jewish community in Sarajevo, known as the *Pinakes*, and the notes kept by those who transcribed the old Serbian Orthodox church books, were singled out by the two readers as highly authentic and valuable material that had never before been used in scholarly research.[14] Andrić's manner of presenting his material, unbiased and objective in tone, was praised; this in itself was felt to add considerable merit to the dissertation. The author's Bosnian background and his unusual literary talent were each recognized as contributing in full measure to the writing of this scholarly work.

Weaknesses were also found. First, the author's use of his mate-

the hands of the Catholic clergy, who have always cherished loyal sympathies for the Sublime Porte."[46] But it was only in 1866 [*sic*], after the proclamation of Hatti-Hümayun and the arrival of Topal Osman-Paša, that a regional (*vilajet*) printing press was established in Sarajevo, which in turn gave birth to the first official gazette, *Bosna*, a weekly. The same press printed the first school primers for the Catholic and Serbian Orthodox schools, likewise the well-known collection of folk songs by B. Petranović.[47] The founding of printing presses followed hard on the heels of the weakening or the outright disintegration of Turkish rule. The Jews of Sarajevo established a press for themselves in 1875; the Jewish community of Belgrade had possessed their own since 1846.[48]

The same pernicious effects of isolation can be seen in other areas of economic life. Isolation is one of the main reasons why Bosnian agriculture, trade, and minor industry languished at a really astonishingly primitive level until quite recently.[49] That this isolation was not limited to material culture can be seen from the ordinance promulgated by Omer-Paša in the year 1851: "Anyone found guilty of having obtained newspapers from foreign Christian countries is at once to be put in heavy chains."[50]

The extremely conservative spirit and intolerance of the native Islamic element hindered the cultural development of the *rayah* even more, if that were possible, than the pressure, the corruption, and the indifference of the Turkish authorities. Not only did this element put up a fight against the reforms being introduced, under pressure from the European powers, by the Porte into Bosnia in the nineteenth century. More broadly, they perceived—and not entirely without reason—in every cultural achievement of the *rayah*, indeed in every change generally, a tendency to alter the whole existing scheme of things and a threat to their own rights and privileges. For example, when in 1850 Tahir-Paša introduced a small bell to call servants in the palace of the vizier, the native Muslims sharply condemned him and openly nicknamed him the *"zvonar"* and the *"kaurin"* [bellringer . . . unbeliever].[51]

Such was the absurd form taken well into recent times by the unwholesome conservatism of these heirs of the Patarins, whose typical representative was the Grand Vizier Mehmed-Paša Sokolović, with his motto,

Nek mi ne sudi Evropa,
jer mogu na štetu njojzi
dignut neprelazan zid
po medji carstva sveg.

(Let me not be provoked by Europe / For I can, to her sorrow, / Raise an insurmountable wall / All down the length of the imperial border.)[52]

Administration

There still remains something to be said about the Turkish administration itself and its effect on the *rayah*.

During the first 150 years of Turkish rule the Bosnian governors (viziers), who themselves were largely from the Bosnian aristocracy, not infrequently displayed interest in the country's progress. With the loot and later proceeds of their great conquests, namely those in Hungary, they erected public buildings and founded endowments (*vakufs*). Most bridges, mosques, caravansaries (public inns), and the like date from this period.[53] During the seventeenth century in Constantinople the Bosnian influence steadily declined. If during the 100-year span just prior to that, Bosnians not only had been governors in their own country but had also attained the rank and dignity of vizier and grand vizier for long stretches of time, now there fell to their lot ever shrinking positions of visibility and influence. Concurrently the great Turkish conquests came to a standstill, and that spelled the end of the vast revenues associated with them. The main sources dried up from which the Bosnian Islamized aristocracy could enrich itself and the first Bosnian governors could erect buildings earmarked for the general welfare.[54]

These changes were decisive. From now on Bosnia's governors were more and more often outlanders who knew neither the language nor the customs of the people. If they wanted to get rich, and most of them did, they could do so now only at the expense of the Bosnian *rayah*. For plunder and conquest no longer were available in a land that found itself in a defensive position. The endowments (*vakufs*), whose existence was tied up with the revenue from Hungary, closed down (e.g., the caravansary in Višegrad). Many landowners (*spahis*) who had to abandon their properties in Hungary returned to Bosnia only to become an increasing burden on their serfs there. It was the beginning of the chaos and legalized lawlessness that lasted to the end of Turkish rule.

Viziers were changed hastily and often. With few exceptions they all, in the short time they held office, tried to convert that office into cash. Their power was further eroded by the distinguished Muslim families who had to be consulted in each important decision if a governor did not wish to turn the discontent against himself. "It became a rule from the eighteenth century on that he convene a kind of council of Bosnian notables to discuss the most important matters."[55] Individual parts of the country were completely under the sway of captains [*kapetani*], a position hereditary in the families of the begs. Until 1850 the imperial viziers had to put up with residing in Travnik, there to "hold well their tongues and exercise the authority over the *rayah* that was not granted them to exercise over the Muslims."[56] Only a few hours' distance from Travnik, all power and administration were in the hands of the beg families and their exercise hung entirely on the good judgment or discretion of these people.[57]

Merely to glance at the history of Bosnia in the last three centuries—based not on Christian sources alone but on Muslim as well— is quite sufficient to form a picture of the viziers appointed by the sultan and to imagine the effect on the *rayah* of their actions and management. Already in 1602 we encounter a governor, Džȩali Hasan-Paša, known as Karajasidži ("Black Writer"), of whom Bašagić himself, in his history written entirely in the Islamic tenor and spirit, says that he was "a notorious robber captain" in Anatolia. When the Turkish authorities found they could not manipulate him, they offered him the governor's post in Bosnia just to get rid of the man. As a result of his brutal tactics all traders, mainly Jews, fled into neighboring countries. Finally, the Bosnian Muslims themselves, unable to tolerate any further the endless fines and other acts of violence, openly rioted against Hasan-Paša. Only in 1605 did the Porte condemn its own governor to death when it discovered that he was secretly negotiating with the pope and the Venetians to sell two Dalmatian towns entrusted to his keeping, Sinj and Herceg Novi.[58]

In 1686, three years after the fall of Ofen [Buda] when Turkish power was beginning to wane, Jegen Osman-Paša was in charge of Bosnia. Bašagić, citing Turkish sources, says of him that instead of remaining in Bosnia he and his henchmen spent the entire period of his governorship "plundering the lands up and down the Danube, troubling himself not at all over the deteriorating state of affairs at home."[59] Bostandži Sulejman-Paša (1754) had two sharpened stakes carried in front of him during his processional entrance into Bosnia to signify his intentions and administrative plans. Among other deeds, "he beat the two Alipašić's so severely with his own two hands that Sulejman-beg died outright while Ali-beg, heavily wounded, nearly failed to recover."[60] At the critical point when the reforms of Abdul Medžid (1844) were about to be carried out in Bosnia, the governor was Osman Nuri-Paša. He is pictured as "a quiet, weak old man who spent the whole livelong day cradling children in the harem and who was so greedy for money that even murder was punished with a fine."[61] Topal Osman-Paša (1865–69), mentioned earlier, was one of the rare governors to show energy, justice, and interest in the country's progress. And yet his own private secretary, Dr. Koetschet, a known Turkophile, admits that "he favored the Muslims and desired nothing less than to equalize the confessions."[62] Martić, who was very close to Osman-Paša, simply called him "the man with all seven deadly sins."[63] Ivan Franjo Jukić called the viziers incompetent, avaricious people unfit for governing.[64] Another Franciscan, Antun Knežević, in his book *Imperial Turkish Governors*, makes an even harsher indictment.[65] What the people thought of the viziers and their administration is suggested by the folk saying, "The best vizier is the one who's ridden out of Constantinople but never ridden into Bosnia."[66]

Turkish corruptibility was proverbial. In this regard it was the viziers who very often set the pace, but since few of them possessed the courage and the force to extort money from the Islamic element of the population, they practiced their craft chiefly upon the *rayah*. The chronicles of the Franciscan monasteries of the last two centuries[67] contain whole columns of sums expended on bribing the viziers and their functionaries, *"ut obturentur ora leonum"* [to stop up the lions' mouths], as the chronicler at Kreševo, Fra Marijan Bogdanović, put it.[68] The often pithy descriptions accompanying the bare figures of fines and extortions display such psychological truth as alone to establish the credibility of these documents.[69] Chronicles and church registers of the other two confessions furnish no less eloquent memoranda. The few surviving notes, sparse though they are, in the Serbian Orthodox monasteries testify to the same facts.[70]

The Jews, though fewer in number, were well-to-do businessmen and profitable targets for extortion.[71] The *Pinakes,* mentioned above as the account books of the Sarajevo Jews, offer a true picture in many ways of conditions as they were then. The year 1730 saw a disbursement of "720 *puli* for the *muteselim,* so as to be spared working Saturdays on the fortification." It was an outlay more than once repeated in the years to come.[72] In 1838, along with many similar entries, the *Pinakes* list the following sums:

Loss on 800 groš sent us by the paša for exchange. . . . 40.–groš

One mirror for Mustafa-Paša. . . . 4.–

Loss on inferior ducats sent us by the paša for exchange[73] . . . .
   8.–

One piece linen, taken by the paša as a sample, not returned[74]
   . . . 50.–

There was always an immense throng of officials and servants in the household of the vizier under assorted titles who kept body and soul together entirely through bribes and fines. But even the administrative and judicial officials (*müsselims* and *kadis*) had no regular salary. On the contrary, they had to lay out considerable sums just to obtain their positions in the first place. These people covered the outlays for their living expenses and replenished the sums paid out for their positions with income from fines and bribes.[75]

Folk tradition even today, in innumerable anecdotes and proverbs, reflects as in a mirror the conditions and legal status of the *rayah* at that period:

For fear of God I mustn't tell lies, for fear of the beg I mustn't tell the truth.	Krivo ne smijem od Boga, a pravo od Bega.
It's hard to become a kadi but once you've made it, butter and honey will come on their own.	Teško je biti kadija, a med i maslo će samo doći.
Woe! to Bosnia so long as there'a a kadi there.	Teško Bosni, dok je u njoj kadija.[76]

The venality that seems to have been a vice of the whole race of Turks showed up from their very first appearance on the stage of history.[77] In the course of time it swelled and grew apace as their power waned, spreading its damaging, demoralizing influence progressively over the whole country. Merely to encounter the authorities meant either humiliation or loss for any Christian. Consequently, from very early times people would avoid stopping off in the towns, seats of administration, just as they shrank from any contact generally with the state organs. Among the *rayah* distrust of the state, indifference to the public good, and doubt in the very possibility of justice on earth became deeply ingrained. In the struggle for existence they had to grasp at antidotes that answered to the medicines employed by their oppressors.[78] In this long drawn-out and unequal struggle the moral attributes of the *rayah* clarified, crystallized, and became fixed, changing for the worse. As a result of Turkish rule the following maxim arose: "Lying is the poor man's stock-in-trade" (*laž je fukarska sermija*).[79] They withdrew from the direct influence of Turkish rule behind the dam of religion, strict custom, and their own kind of life, hard and utterly unassuming. In one sense, then, the Turks had "only a superficial effect" on the *rayah*, but their indirect influence through law and administration was extremely powerful and equally negative, whether one speaks of its material or its spiritual impact.

All researchers into Bosnia and its past, be they Serbo-Croatian or foreign, have felt in a position to state in concert and more or less forcefully that the effect of Turkish rule was absolutely negative. One of the few who would hope to detect positive facts of some sort in the Turkish influence on Bosnia could digest them all into the following, single sentence: "The world of the Turks thus brought its blessings to the southern Slavs in two ways, first by forcing them into a desperate battle for existence and second by acquainting them with Arabic and Persian industry and craftsmanship."[80] The logical nonsense and psychological absurdity of the first part of this statement—to talk of enforced struggle as a positive service of the Turks—absolves us from any need to discuss it. The second part, after all that has been said, can be acceptable only to superficial observers and lovers of the picturesque and the strange.

The Turks could bring no cultural content or sense of higher historic mission, even to those South Slavs who accepted Islam; for their Christian subjects, their hegemony brutalized custom and meant a step to the rear in every respect.

4 The Spiritual and Intellectual Life of the Catholic Populace Under the Turks in Its Characteristic Embodiment: The Literary and Cultural Work of the Franciscans

History of the Franciscans in Bosnia

The first Catholic missionaries in Patarin Bosnia were members of the Dominican order, but these soon were replaced by Franciscans. The Bosnian vicariate founded by Fra Geraldo Odonis was already in existence by about 1340.[1]

At that time in Bosnia Catholics consisted exclusively of immigrant miners—Germans (Saxons) or Dalmatian Latins [*Romanen*]. Such being the case, the first Franciscans to be called upon for the pastoral care of these foreigners naturally belonged to the same racial groups. But since the Franciscans early expanded into the missionary field and began to convert Patarins and members of the Orthodox church, they were forced to learn the language of the country where they worked and from the very start had to be concerned for their successor generations among the native population.[2]

Under the last two kings the Franciscans, as the only Catholic priests in Bosnia, enjoyed both increasing respect and saw their numbers rise markedly. It was to their influence that they ascribed the conversion of the last king but one, Stjepan Toma.[3] On the eve of invasion by the Turks the Bosnian vicariate, in addition to today's Bosnia and Hercegovina, included almost all of modern Croatia, Slavonia, and Dalmatia and part of Albania and was subdivided into eight jurisdictions. There were many monasteries and rectories, although their number cannot be determined precisely any more than can the sum total of Franciscans themselves. By that point the majority of these stemmed from Bosnia itself or its neighbors; but they also came in part from Italy.[4]

The Turkish invasion brought about not only the fall of the Bosnian kingdom but with it the collapse of the Catholic church organization. About thirty-two monasteries and rectories were destroyed at that time. The Franciscans fled along with some of the nobility and peasants, everybody trying to save as many church vestments and as much property as he or she could. (Included was the body of Saint Luke, which until then had been kept in Jajce and was known and venerated as a relic throughout Christendom.)[5]

Not all Franciscans left the country, however. Batinić writes that when Sultan Mehmed II, "the Conqueror," was about to depart Bosnia in 1464, Fra Angelus Zvjezdović appeared before him:

> The soldiers led in Fra Angelus and he implored protection for the Franciscans and the Catholic church. Realizing that the land lay waste and uncared for and that the Franciscans could be used as a tool to restore normal conditions and to bring about the pacification of the country, the sultan displayed a benevolent and sympathetic attitude and issued to them the famous Ahd-Name (writ of protection).

This document informs all and sundry, "nobles and non-nobles alike," that the sultan is particularly well disposed toward "the Bosnian clergy." At the same time orders are given that no difficulties shall be created, either for those priests who stayed in place or for those who had left the country only to return, nor for their churches, "so long as they shall remain loyal to me and my commands." Upon all this the sultan took a "most solemn oath."[6]

However, if the Franciscans did not long remain loyal, neither, as we shall see shortly, was the sultan's promise kept.

A natural consequence of the conquest of Bosnia was that those portions of the vicariate that were to remain under Christian administration had sooner or later to leave it. This happened first in 1468 with Dubrovnik (Ragusa), followed by Croatia in 1514.[7]

In this manner the Franciscan province of Bosnia Argentina (*Bosna Srebrena*) arose under Turkish hegemony. It was in *Bosna Srebrena* that there evolved a distinct type, the Bosnian Franciscan, whose cultural and literary efforts are discussed below.

It would appear that during the first decades of Turkish rule life was half tolerable for Christians and that the Turkish authorities, so far as the Franciscans were concerned, held to the directives of the Ahd-

Name of Sultan Mehmed II. It was the first half of the next century, the sixteenth, that saw the beginnings of persecution, including the destruction of Franciscan monasteries.[8] Those priests especially were harassed who entered Bosnia from Christian countries. For this reason, throughout the sixteenth century the Franciscans begged the pope repeatedly to appoint a bishop from their own ranks. In the year 1573 Fra Anton Matković was designated Bishop of Bosnia by the pope, and in the course of time a long series of Bosnian Franciscans was elevated to that rank. The position of these bishops was exceedingly difficult, not only owing to unpleasant conditions under the Turks but also because of the Franciscans themselves, with whom the bishops kept coming into conflict.[9]

Despite all difficulties the province of Bosnia Argentina possessed, toward the end of the sixteenth century (1591), sixteen monasteries. Of these, six lay in Dalmatia and Slavonia and ten in Bosnia proper. (The Slavonian and Dalmatian cloisters had again been taken over by the Franciscans as Turkish conquest inexorably proceeded.) The number of monks was very small and the number of priests— thirty-one altogether in the sixteen monasteries—shockingly so. During the period of the great Turkish conquests, up to the middle of the seventeenth century, the Bosnian Franciscans followed the Turks everywhere into all the conquered districts, there to be the exclusive caretakers of their people's spiritual well-being in the absence of the secular clergy, who had withdrawn before the advancing Turks. And in the major battles in Slavonia and Dalmatia, the Franciscans also took an active part.[10]

The natural consequence was that the Turks turned violently against the Bosnian Franciscans and their monasteries, especially after becoming embittered by ensuing failures. To no avail did the sultans, Süleyman the Magnificent and his successors, reconfirm and strengthen the rights granted the Franciscans in the Ahd-Name.[11]

Incessant harassment and money fines forced the Franciscans to abandon their monasteries, one after the other. And persecutions and wars, particularly the advance of Prince Eugene of Savoy in 1697, precipitated the abandonment of Bosnia by a segment of the Catholic populace. And with it went the Franciscans. By the beginning of the seventeenth [sic] century there were only four Franciscan monasteries left in Bosnia, with twenty-six monks and lay brothers.[12] This whole century stood under the sign of perpetual struggle against need, pestilence, and hunger (especially in the year 1782), and it was equally characterized by violence and repression on the part of the Turkish authorities.[13]

After the energetic bishop Fra Nikola Ogramić died in 1701, the cathedral chair of Bosnia in Djakovo was no longer occupied by Franciscans but by secular bishops from Croatia (Patačić, Bakić, etc.). These men, however, did not dare step onto Bosnian soil. Upon repeated complaints by the Franciscans that they had not laid eyes on a bishop in their land for decades, the Holy See finally appointed as apostolic vicar of Bosnia in 1735 Fra Matija Delivić. That same year, 1735, Dalmatia separated from Bosnia, becoming an independent Franciscan province. In 1757 an independent Franciscan province of St. Ivan Kapistran was founded for the area to the north of the Sava, compared to which Bosnia formed merely a custody. In light of this arrangement, which "hurt and embittered them to the utmost," the Bosnian Franciscans sent one of their most respected members, Fra Philipp [*Filip*] Laštrić, to Rome. Laštrić succeeded in getting Bosnia Argentina once again proclaimed an autonomous province (in 1758).

From as early as the sixteenth century the Orthodox patriarchs of Peć had aimed at bringing all Christians of Serbian nationality under their jurisdiction, no matter what their confession. For almost three hundred years Greek patriarchs and bishops repeatedly tried to impose on Bosnian Franciscans and their faithful the same taxes that were paid by the Serbian Orthodox clergy with their population. They justified their claims with firmans granted them by different sultans stating that all Christians within range of the Turkish empire should be under their authority.[14]

Taking the opposite view, the Franciscans appealed to the contents of the 1464 Ahd-Name and to the fact that they, who were of the Latin Rite, could not be subject to the Orthodox patriarch. "We belong to the Latin religion," they would say, and even, "We are Hungarian!"[15] Bitter fights and prolonged, costly lawsuits before the viziers over these claims lasted to the end of the eighteenth century and cost the Franciscans much money and effort, not to speak of the moral aftereffects of all this discord, which only served to enlarge the already deep rift between the adherents of the two confessions, Catholic and Orthodox.[16]

In the nineteenth century Bosnia was the scene of particularly stormy political events. Franciscans rarely participated actively in them but had to put up with their nasty consequences. Throughout the Serbian uprisings they were at pains to keep the Catholic element calm, however much they may have wanted "in spirit," as always, a victory for Christian arms.[17] But the aftermath of the Christian revolts against the Turkish empire—redoubled hatred for Christians on the part of Muslims, anarchy, violence by Turkish soldiers, inflation, and hunger—these, the Franciscans also had to share in full measure.[18] Like other Christians, Franciscans took no part in the prolonged and bloody fights waged by the Bosnian Muslims in the first half of the nineteenth century against the reforms and governors of the sultan. They had nothing to hope for from either of the contesting factions. Still, they were often implicated and had to take the results.

Bosnian Franciscans also participated in political and intellectual movements beyond the Sava during that century.

Internal life in the Bosnian Franciscan province was no less lively. The rising generation of Franciscans was trained in two different countries. Some took their educational nourishment in Italy, others in Hungary and Croatia with the help of the Kaiser Joseph endowment and the generous support of Bishop Ožegović and Count Nugent [Nižan]. This education in two diverse spheres generated two diverse mentalities among the Bosnian Franciscans. Those who returned from their studies in Hungary (the "Hungarians") brought back ideas of the Enlightenment in the spirit of Joseph and, later, "Illyrian" notions of a national rebirth; their whole education took on a more national character. The ones from the Papal State ("Italians"), on the other hand, spearheaded by Fra Rafael Barišić, were averse to any nationalism and strove to discipline the Bosnian Franciscans "in the spirit of Roman politics."[19]

The struggle between Bishop Barišić and the majority of the Franciscans lasted an exceedingly long time and was so harsh that it often took very coarse and unedifying forms. Not only did Rome intervene but Vienna and Constantinople as well. The resulting friction culminated in Bosnia Argentina's suspension as a province—temporarily—in 1843. Only in 1847 was its status restored by Pope Pius IX. This struggle, which we cannot go into here in detail, was in many respects highly characteristic not just of the psychology of Bosnian Franciscans but in general of the relationship between South Slav Catholics and Rome.[20]

With Bosnia's occupation by the Austro-Hungarian monarchy in 1878 and the establishment of normal social and ecclesiastical conditions, the historic mission of the Bosnian Franciscans came to an end.

Conditions Shaping Bosnian Franciscan Development

The conditions we sought to depict in the foregoing chapters, both when Bosnia was still independent and during the four hundred years of Turkish rule, shaped the character of the Bosnian Franciscan encountered throughout its history. Environment conditioned his activity, creating a special type within the order, as within the clergy generally of the Roman Catholic church.

Although the Franciscan mission in Bosnia was to do battle with the Patarin faith—and it was a mission most zealously pursued— Franciscans could not very well disavow their own lineage and often revealed in the course of duty attributes rather similar to those of their countrymen and opponents in faith, "the good Bosnians." The thirst for spiritual autonomy, a tendency to be refractory, a certain exclusivity, a taste for xenophobia, all these traits found eloquent expression in their relationship to the highest powers of the church and to the Catholic clergy of other regions.[21]

To judge by the nearly unanimous testimony of the official visitors sent out by the church, the Bosnian Franciscans could serve all the world as a shining example of Catholic spirituality, in view of their willingness to make sacrifices and their perseverance in their ministry, the faultless lives they led, and the mighty influence they exerted on the faithful. With a self-denial that bordered on martyrdom, they defended and maintained the leading position of the Roman Catholic church in the Balkans. And yet when it came to upholding the "rights of their Mother Province," Bosnia Argentina, they resisted "Roman justice" openly and tenaciously, doing battle with bishops and secular clergy alike in a stiff-necked way that vividly recalls the struggles of the Bosnian Patarins. Their determination to keep the Cyrillic alphabet is seen by Prohaska as a "Bogomil inheritance."[22]

But the effects of rule by the Turks on the Franciscans, on the scope of their activity, were much more immediate and visible than this. The pressure of that rule lasted so long and was so strong that even such universal and disciplined organizations as the Catholic church and the Franciscan order had to bend to it and, wittingly or unwittingly, intentionally or not, to change their patterns.

Already by the middle of the sixteenth century the Franciscans were beginning to wear common peasant clothes to avoid persecution. On their travels through the widely scattered settlements they would stay for weeks on end in peasant huts. To keep their presence a secret from the Turks, the people addressed them not as priests but as "Uncle" (*ujak*), an expression still current among the common folk.[23] While they and their flock thus tightened their mutual and ever more intimate embrace, by the same token Franciscans could not adhere to the rules of their order with regard to clothes, food, accommodation, and general life-style.[24] So on many points those regulations had to be more or less modified, "*secundum mores et regiones.*"

In 1625 Pope Urban VIII granted the Franciscans the right to own land and work it, in recognition of the exceptional circumstances under which they had to live.[25] Not only did they carry weapons (permitted by the Turkish authorities in special firmans),[26] but they were often compelled by circumstances to use them.[27]

When in 1850 the hated practice of tax farming was abolished the government ordered the clergy of the different religions to collect the taxes from their own faithful. In the people's interest the Franciscans were glad to comply, although they knew that this activity violated the basic rules of their order. ("*Cum hoc statui nostro e diametro sit oppositum.*")[28]

The regulations, however, of the Franciscan order were not all that was affected by Turkish hegemony. The conditions discussed in the previous chapter were ever more keenly felt by the Franciscans as champions of the Catholic *rayah*. They had to employ bribery and "cunning" to win the most trifling advantage; they had to use secret paths when they traveled about, as indeed in all their affairs ("*vanno sempre per le strade secrete*"); in "spirit" ever on the side of the Christian deliverers, they had to pretend the opposite; and so forth. Hence their work, side by side with its many virtues and great merit, also reveals mistakes and shortcomings that cannot be ignored.[29]

One such blemish on their record is that out of their own religious zeal they worked to destroy established customs and popular traditions. Until quite recent times Franciscans have been quite indifferent to the value of safeguarding the treasury of folk songs and tales, even attempting, in fact, to root these out entirely among the people.[30] Nonetheless, over their 600 years of work in Bosnia they have provided a rare and beautiful picture of cultural labor and Christian sacrifice. It is due solely to Franciscan efforts that Bosnia under the Turks saw any literary activity at all, and if it did serve chiefly church purposes and is of only historical value to us, it nevertheless represents the fruit of noble effort. It can be appreciated at its true value only by taking into account the conditions under which it came about.

Franciscan Literature

Works to Edify and Educate

Under the Turks the Franciscans were the sole representatives of Serbo-Croatian literature in Bosnia.* The Serbian Orthodox clergy, which was under the pernicious control of Greek patriarchs and bishops and had no support from any foreign Christian power until the eighteenth century, could not pursue literary activity at all because of its poverty and minimal education. This left the sector of the population that had converted to Islam entirely dependent on literary productions in Turkish (Arabian and Persian, as the case may be), hence without access to the Serbo-Croatian linguistic sphere and Western culture.

While a lively literary tradition had developed in the sixteenth century, first in Dalmatia and then in Croatia, there is not a trace of any such literary initiatives in Bosnia. The reasons are clear enough from what has been said already. Only at the start of the seventeenth century are the first stirrings of a Franciscan literature detectable. The stimulus, predictably, came from the outside.

---

*The following arguments rest on the statements in Jelenić, *Kultura i Bosanski Franjevci*, II: 433–592; and Prohaska, Schrifttum, 93–146.

Urged onward by the desire to employ the same means that the Reformation had so successfully employed (that is, to write in the manner and language of the people), the Roman Catholic church, following the resolutions of the Council of Trent (1545–63), began to disseminate its teachings among all ranks of the people in whatever form and language would be most accessible to any given group.[31] The entire body of Catholic writing in Bosnia developed along that guideline and with that end in view up until the nineteenth century.

This first period was opened by the Franciscan Matija Divković (1563–1631). Living as a priest in Sarajevo, he began to write with the aim of spreading Catholic teachings among the people. His work consisted, naturally, only in copying, translating, and summarizing ("*ispisa, privede, i složi*").

Those were the years when the Spanish Jesuit Jakob Ledesma and Cardinal Roberto Bellarmino were at the height of their reputation, each working in the spirit of the Council of Trent.[32] Divković produced some translations of these men as well as something of the German Dominican Johann von Heisterbach, adjusting both text and style to the people for whom they were intended. The older Glagolitic literature also served as a source and model for him.[33] He published his works in Venice and, since there was no press with a Cyrillic font, cast the letters himself.[34] Thus the year 1611 saw Divković's *Christian Teaching* and *One Hundred Miracles* appear in Venice.[35] In 1616 he published, again in Venice, a new and enlarged edition of the former plus a book of sermons.[36]

The alphabet used by Divković was the so-called Bosnian Cyrillic script. Basically it was a cursive type of the common Cyrillic in whose development the Glagolitic and Roman alphabets had a minor role.[37] It was the script used for documents from the earliest days of Bosnian history by the ruling sovereigns and by all three confessions. Being as well the only script that at least some few of the population could read, for that reason alone it suited the church's need to spread its teachings "*in carettere serviano*," as it took a defensive stand against Protestantism.[38] In the course of time, when this need was no longer so pressing, the Cyrillic alphabet ceased to be employed by the church, although the Franciscans stood up for their "beloved alphabet" with the conservative tenacity characteristic of them on any issue.[39] Even at the dawn of the nineteenth century and all the way up to Gaj's reform, they were still lamenting the loss of the "old special letters of our Illyrian or Slavic language" and complaining that it was "hard to write every word of our tongue with its own peculiarities in a foreign alphabet."[40] They did try, as we shall see, to adapt the Roman alphabet to their language and looked for possibilities of expressing each sound of Serbo-Croatian. Gaj's reform put an end to these futile efforts at eliminating the "Babelonian confusion" of Roman orthography. But the reform spelled Cyrillic's final demise among the Bosnian Catholics.

Even though Divković's work offers nothing original and has long been of mere historic interest, it was of great value for Bosnia's intellectual [geistig] life, not just because he inaugurated a line of religious writers but because this "poor, little brother, rich in longing and love," as he styled himself, had something in his character that was good and noble and strove for education and progress.

Other Franciscans having the same goals and methods followed the way paved by Divković, the "pious theologian." Stjepan Matijević from Tuzla (a Salinis) translated in 1630 from Italian a little book about confession.[41] Pavao Posilović, like Divković one of the most popular Franciscan writers, left two works written in the Italian manner of the day. Born in Glamoč, appointed Bishop of Scardona (Skradin) in 1642, he pursued the same aims as his predecessors: to teach his flock "how to live righteously and die in the Lord."[42] Both works appeared in several editions, the later ones—in the eighteenth century—being printed already in Roman script. Pavao Papić, a contemporary of Posilović and a very highly respected member of the Bosnian Franciscan province, translated the Italian work, Le sette trombe.[43]

The sole example of Bosnian literature of that period not serving immediate religious needs is a poem composed by August Vlastelinović from Sarajevo in honor of his uncle, Bishop Jerolim Lukić—occasional verse. He had it printed in Rome, and in Cyrillic.[44]

Stjepan Markovac, or Margitić, is the last writer to use Cyrillic letters. In his time, the beginning of the seventeenth century, the Roman alphabet was progressively making its own way and a gap was beginning to form between those Franciscans who used Latin letters and wrote in a "learned" manner and those who took Divković as their model and used Cyrillic letters in order to remain "ethnic." Margitić published two books, The Christian Confession and In Praise of the Saints.[45] The first of these was reprinted a number of times up to 1842, winning great popularity under the title *Stjepanuša* [The Book of Stephen].

Next to the Bosnian literature in Cyrillic, there developed a literature in the Roman alphabet. Fra Ivan Bandulović of Skoplje (southwestern Bosnia), a contemporary of Divković, wrote *Epistles and Gospels for the Whole Year.*[46] The book is based upon an older collection of epistles and gospels published in 1546 in Venice by the Dalmatian clergyman Don Benedat Zborovčić. In the writing of Bandulović there is a marked discrepancy between the Čakavian and Štokavian dialects.

Fra Ivan Ančić, or Johannes Anitius (Anicio), as he called himself in his Latin works, gained the reputation of being a learned writer and teacher in Italy, where he died in the year 1685. Of his works written in Serbo-Croatian, Prohaska knows only *Ogledalo misničko,*[47] while Jelenić cites two further works.[48] Ančić is also interesting because he was the first Bosnian writer of that time to try and achieve a more truthful representation of the sounds of the Serbo-Croatian language by combining Roman letters.[49]

Although he did not come from Bosnia but from Dalmatia, Fra Toma Babić gained great popularity among the Bosnian Catholics with his work *Blooms of Diverse Churchly Fragrances.*[50] This work was more than once reprinted and copied. Several Franciscan writers enlarged and supplemented it with new additions, so that it became "an encyclopedic repository of the most popular pieces of religious writing."[51] In this form and under the well-known name *Babuše* [Books of Babić] his work was known and loved up to the nineteenth century as the only reading material and spiritual nourishment in the Catholic homes of Bosnia.

Fra Lovro Sitović from Ljubuški was the son of Muslim parents. (When just a small child he was left behind by his father as a hostage with a Christian from Dalmatia. There he became acquainted with Christianity and learned to love it. Later, after having returned to his parental home, he fled, was baptized, and became a Franciscan monk.) In addition to a Latin-Illyrian grammar (Venice, 1712), Sitović published a book on Christian dogma, *Christian Teaching* (*Nauk Krstjanski,* Buda, 1734). But his most interesting work is his *Song of Hell* [*Pisna od Pakla; Das Lied Über die Hölle*],[52] in which he declaims passionately against folk songs and their unchristian heroes, their praise of love, wine, and so forth. He appeals to the clergy to stamp out among the people the singing of such songs, frivolous and detrimental to the soul, and to circulate ones that call for devotion and penitence (such as his own *Song of Hell*, "which deals especially with hellfire, darkness, and eternity"). Sitović himself, however, composed his song in the ten-syllable verse form of the folk song. It differs from the real verses of folk poetry only in being frequently irregular and quite devoid of any beauty.

Fra Filip Laštrić from Očevje was both an outstanding representative of his order and a defender of the rights of that order's province. In addition, he was remarkable for his literary activities. When the province of Bosnia Argentina was in the process of being divided, Laštrić was sent to Vienna and Rome. In 1758 he succeeded in having the pope return to Bosnia its former rights as an autonomous province and grant it once again primacy over the Hungarian province of St. John Kapistran. By his Bosnian brethren he was given the title of "Savior and Restorer of the Province" [*Spasitelj i obnovitelj provincije*].[53] Laštrić wrote down a defense of the rights of his province in *Epitome Vetustatis* [*sic*].[54] He also composed three books of sermons "for Bosnian priests and missionaries."[55] In 1766, at the request of "the spiritual shepherds of simple folk," he published a new, shortened, and simplified version of his sermons under the title *Nediglnik Dvostruk*. Laštrić also helped put together, as co-author, the well-known work of Daniele Farlati, *Illyricum sacrum*.

Fra Jerolim Filipović was the author of a very popular and solid book of Christian doctrine [*Nauk krstjanski*].[56] Fra Marko Dobretić-Jezerčić and Fra Luka Vladimirović left works whose content was moral theology, and Vincenc Vicić left a book of hymns. Bishops Fra Grgo Ilić and Fra Augustin Miletić, though appearing indeed in the nineteenth century, nevertheless belong in the list of religious writers of Bosnia enumerated here because of the spirit of their works.

To conclude this period, we ought to mention at least by name those Bosnians who, having fled the Turks, worked abroad but whose literary activity had some meaning for their country. Foremost among them is one already mentioned, Fra Juraj Dobretić, or Dragišić, who was known and appreciated in Italy as a writer on theology (Georgius Benignus de Salviatis). He fell into a conflict with the church authorities because of his defense of Savonarola and of the noncanonic (Hebrew) books. After a stay of thirty years in Italy, he returned to Bosnia but could not adjust to the alien circumstances of his homeland, returned via Dubrovnik to Italy, and finally died there in 1520 as the bishop of Barletta.[57]

Ivan Tomko Mrnjavić was likewise a writer in exile and likewise wrote a book on Christian dogma. He also turned out some epic and dramatic works based on Italian models and in the spirit of the times.[58] Mrnjavić was an honorary citizen of Rome, held high church honors and positions, and was appointed the bishop of Bosnia in 1631. But since he was "not used to dealing with Turks" he never dared step onto Bosnian soil.[59]

In Dubrovnik (Ragusa) there lived yet another emigrant, another "writer and ancestor-dreamer." This was Juraj Radojević Gizdelin, who styled himself "Vojvoda" and "Prince [Knez] of Bosnia" and who published in 1686 in Venice a long poem about the siege of Ofen [Buda] in that year and the victory over the Turks by the troops of Emperor Leopold I.[60]

The beginning of the nineteenth century saw the end of this kind of Bosnian Franciscan literature. It was replaced by a new literary-political movement with new ideas and new goals.

In the 200 years of its flowering the Bosnian Franciscans produced neither original nor deep nor well-structured works. But that had not been their aim, which was to "serve the spiritual salvation of Christian folk and be their solace." Given the goal, it was fully achieved. Further, this Franciscan writing could take sole credit for seeing that Bosnian Catholic spiritual life developed strictly in accordance with the religious and moral precepts of the Roman Catholic church.[61] As in everything the Franciscans did, so also in their literature one can detect the rivalry, now latent, now open, between native Bosnian elements nourished by the living spring of colloquial speech and using the national script, on the one hand, and "Italian" elements that were "learned," talked "elegantly," and believed that any idiosyncrasy in spirit, language, or writing had to be sacrificed on the altar of church universality.

In Service to the Enlightenment

Clearly, Franciscan religious literature in its first period extended into the early decades of the nineteenth century. But for all Bosnia's backwardness, despite all the measures taken by the Turks, whether willful or unplanned, to keep the population isolated from the Christian countries at its borders, the restless nineteenth century with its ideas of liberty and progress knocked on its doors as well.

The Franciscans, who from the start of the seventeenth century had served the ideas of the Council of Trent with so much devotion, now placed themselves at the service of these new ideas. Their young members, returning from studies in Hungary (Veszprem, Budapest, Stuhlweissenburg), brought with them the fructifying idea of national rebirth, which had taken hold among the Croats and the Serbs north of the Sava and which was advancing with vigor.

When Ljudevit Gaj in December 1835 printed his call to "Illyria" and soon thereafter transformed "Danicza Horvatzka Slavonzka y Dalmatinzka" into "Danica ilirska" [1836], the Franciscans at once became his enthusiastic collaborators. They appear for the most part as poets, but they also worked as political correspondents for Gaj's newspaper *Ilirske narodne novine*.

Influenced by this movement, Franciscans began collecting folk songs and tales, hitherto much neglected. Ivan Franjo Jukić, under the pseudonym Slavoljub Bošnjak, published his *Zemljopis i poviestnica Bosne* in Zagreb [1851], dedicating it to Ljudevit Gaj. All the work of the Franciscans at that time, not excluding their strenuous conflict with Bishop Barišić, took place under the sign of the star and the half moon, the Illyrian emblem.[62] From that moment, thanks to the Franciscans and their work both literary and cultural-political, Bosnia never again lost its spiritual connection with neighboring countries sharing the same language.

The first "Illyrian" from Bosnia to answer Gaj's call was Fra Martin Nedić. Nedić was born in 1810 in Tolisa, studied theology in Hungary, and later performed important functions in the Bosnian Franciscan province. This "first man from Bosnia" (to use his words) responded to the call with a long poem in the folk song's ten-syllable verse form, only in rhyme. Its title was, "A Discourse Among Illyrian Vilas in the Spring of 1835."[63] The archive of the Franciscan monastery at Tolisa has a manuscript of a second work by Nedić, "Discourse of the Vilas in the Spring of 1841" [*Razgovor vilah u premalitje 1841*].[64]

Thereafter Nedić kept a kind of versified chronicle. With his collaborator Fra Marijan Šunjić he sang of Jelačić's campaign against the

Magyars,[65] described in lengthy poems the defeat of the Bosnian Muslim oligarchy in its battle against the reforms coming out of Constantinople, and celebrated the revolt of the *rayah* against the Turks.[66] He died in 1895.

In Fra Franjo Ivan [*sic*] Jukić we encounter a personality essentially different in function and kind from that of his contemporaries and collaborators, one revealed in both action and writing. By contrast with the other Franciscan writers, Jukić had a revolutionary mind, unbridled and sharp. Yet at the same time he was inventive and persevering. He was entirely given over to zeal on behalf of his people, as though filled by some apostolic mission. Intellectually gifted and physically strong, during his short life Jukić was steadily motivated by the thought of "bringing the simple people out of the darkness of ignorance into the light of truth." In pursuit of this goal he was active in several areas. The results were uneven, but always demonstrated an eagerness and self-sacrifice that fill us with admiration.

Jukić was born in Banja Luka in 1818 and studied theology in Veszprem, Hungary. When just a cleric he fled with a few friends from Veszprem to Bosnia "in order to start a revolt against the Turks there." Older Franciscans dissuaded them from pursuing this youthful folly. After completing his studies, Jukić worked for a few years as a chaplain and priest, in the latter capacity founding a school in Varcar.[67] In 1850 he initiated a broadly based, combined fund drive among Bosnian Catholics and members of the Orthodox church for the establishment of schools, in a printed appeal calling upon all Christians in Bosnia. The undertaking miscarried owing to a lack of understanding.

Jukić's literary output was far-reaching and varied. Already in 1838 he was sending Gaj poems for the *Danica*. While still a student he reported that he was ready with a book of stories and moreover that he had prepared the works of the Ragusan poets Menčetić and Držić for publication. None of these ever appeared in print, and none is completely extant. With the exception of a few fragments that appeared in the *Danica* or the *Bosanski Prijatelj*, all of them were lost as a result of the stormy, unsettled life of their author.

Jukić's activities in the scientific-organizational domain were more successful, more comprehensive, and more important. In 1847, together with a few young Franciscans, he issued a "Call to Join the Bosnian Circle" [*Poziv u Kolo bosansko*]. This circle was intended to be a kind of literary-cultural association with the aim of publishing a newspaper (*Bosanski Svetogled*) and of establishing schools.

To the practical, seasoned, and conservative Franciscans who were entrusted with administering the province of Bosnia in those meager and trying times, this young enthusiast's initiative seemed too risky, too unlikely. So they withheld the *"exequatur,"* denying him the necessary permission. And his venture failed. But Jukić could find no peace. In Zagreb in 1850 he succeeded in publishing at Gaj's expense the first installment of his magazine "Friend of Bosnia" [*Bosanski Prijatelj*]. There he complained about the lack of understanding on the part of his Bosnian brothers and about their passivity. The following year he brought out, this time at his own expense, a second volume of *Bosanski Prijatelj*, which he dedicated to Omer-Paša Latas. In that same year, 1851, his *Bosnian Geography and History [Zemljopis i poviestnica Bosne]* was published at the press of Ljudevit Gaj.[68] As a supplement to this work Jukić printed "Wishes and Entreaties of Christians in Bosnia and Hercegovina" [*Želje i molbe kristjana u Bosni i Hercegovini*]. In unprecedented fashion the document demanded of the sultan a whole series of reforms in favor of the Bosnian Christians. It was an act of audacity that cost the author his freedom and his life. Omer-Paša, Jukić's onetime protector, had him arrested and transferred to Constantinople. There he was set free and banished to Rome, but only "so that the pope would bridle and curb him." From Rome Jukić turned first to Dubrovnik, then to Djakovo where he lived with Bishop Strossmayer, in great physical pain and consumed with longing for his homeland. He died in 1857 in Vienna, where he had gone for medical help.

Apart from the works mentioned, Jukić published in the *Danica ilirska* and the *Serbsko-dalmatinski Magazin* a long series of travel descriptions and historical-geographical works.[69]

Jukić's belletristic activity may be of no literary value, his scientific works long out of date, and his collections of folk poetry lacking in method and definite plan. Yet the fact that he undertook much and that he strove mightily—his personality taken as a whole—entitles Jukić to a place among the significant men in nineteenth-century Balkan history, men who in the most trying of times and at great personal sacrifice were honestly doing their best to create an improved environment with greater dignity in the future for Christians within the Ottoman Empire.

More productive and more systematic was the literary activity of Jukić's contemporary, Fra Grgo Martić. Martić, born in 1822 in Posušje, studied first in the monastery of Kreševo, later being sent off to Zagreb and Stuhlweissenburg [Stoni Biograd] for further work. He spent most of his life as a priest in Sarajevo where, nominally in charge of the Franciscan agency, he was in effect entrusted with representing not only the Franciscans but all Catholics in Bosnia. Skilled in languages, adroit and quick, active and diplomatic at all times, Martić knew how to stay on the best of terms with foreign consuls and the viceroys of the sultan alike, thus maximizing the benefit for his order and all the faithful. Not till after 1878 did he leave Sarajevo and retire to Kreševo. There, in the monastery, he died in 1906, deep in old age, esteemed by both church and state and honored by the entire cultural establishment.

Martić too came in touch with the Illyrians in Zagreb. His first poems are imbued with their spirit. When Jukić printed the first number of *Bosanski Prijatelj*, Martić was his chief collaborator. Martić's major effort is *"Osvetnici"* [The Avengers]. In seven volumes of verse it celebrates the uprisings of the *rayah* in Hercegovina and Montenegro up to 1878.[70] But he was gifted with exceptional creative facility and wrote, besides, many thousands of verses. Among other pieces, he left an attempted epic on Kosovo. Another, the *"Osmanida,"* was lost. (He had hidden it from the Turkish authorities in a granary but once all danger had passed found only "tiny bits of paper—mice had chewed it up.")[71] He also wrote a *Geography Primer for Bosnia's Catholic Schools* [*Početni zemljopis za Katoličke učione u Bosni; Geographie für Anfänger, zum Gebrauche in den Katolischen Schulen in Bosnien*, Sarajevo, 1871]. Finally, his memoirs [*Zapamćenja*] were published in Zagreb in 1906 by the historian F. Šišić.

Martić wrote in the decasyllabic verse form of the folk song and employed a diction that was at once rich and pure yet so artificially folksy that it seems stilted and unclear. In his time "The Avengers" was thought to be the equal of Mažuranić's *"Smrt Smail-age Čengića"* [The Death of Smail Aga Čengić] and Martić was touted as the "Christian Homer" and a poet "of the first rank."[72] Clear to anyone today is that he was overestimated by his contemporaries. Literary and political conditions brought him fame as a poet that would never have been his under different circumstances.

The rich and powerful language that Martić possessed as his birthright was in itself reason enough for an honored position in literature at that time. Folk poetry's form and tone cast a magic spell over temperaments still inclined toward Romanticism. And the theme, deliverance of Christians from the yoke of the Turks, reflected a mood that was national, universal, political. Bosnia in those years was the focus of general attention and Martić became its spiritual representative. Therefore was he honored—and overrated.

Fra Anton Knežević, Jukić's epigone, published *Krvava knjiga* [Book of Blood] in Zagreb in 1869 about acts of violence by the Turkish authorities in Bosnia. He wrote several other historical works containing lively descriptions but lacking in discernment and inappropriate to the times.[73] And, completely in the spirit of Jukić, he edited yet a fourth volume of *Bosanski Prijatelj*.

Bishop Fra Marijan Šunjić (1798–1880), a student of Mezzofanti, was another who concerned himself with poetry, history, and philology. He deserves merit as a collector of folk songs and a founder of schools.[74]

Fra Petar Bakula was a writer of chronicles and a poet (1816–73).

Such are the Franciscan writers of the second period who owed their prominence to the bigger, more voluminous works. Apart from them a considerable number of Bosnian Franciscans of that period also participated in the literary life of the time with lesser works. And then, last, there were those who composed and printed theological tracts in Latin or occasional poetry.[75]

The Significance of Franciscan Literature

Franciscan writers of the nineteenth century as a rule employed the meter of folk song. They frequently enjoyed drawing on characters from folk poetry. Their language was rich and lively even though one notices how the *ikavian* and *ijekavian* dialects struggled for the upper hand. The Cyrillic alphabet was gone for good.[76]

If during the seventeenth and eighteenth centuries the Franciscans generally had their works printed in Venice, during the nineteenth century the center of printing moved to Zagreb. If the literature of the first two centuries was purely religious and came about solely at the initiative of the church authorities under whose supervision it then developed, the Franciscan literature of the nineteenth century wholly served ideas of a national rebirth and deliverance from the Turkish yoke. And it developed without the cooperation, and often against the will, of the church.

The literature of the second period did not achieve the same circulation and influence among the people as that of the first period. It lost its way, like the whole Illyrian movement whose reflection it was, in bombastic patriotism that led nowhere, without concrete and achievable goals.

And yet this Franciscan literature was of great significance for the country's spiritual and intellectual life. It is simply that the merit is more noticeable in the cultural-political domain than in belles lettres. Thanks largely to the Franciscans' activity as writers, the disastrous isolation with which Turkish administration surrounded Bosnia was breached. This most backward of the South Slavic lands now could mediate the intellectual products of its more progressive neighbors. On the other hand, through their literature, the Franciscans made the South Slavic culture centers, especially Zagreb, aware of Bosnia and its primitive but interesting forms of spiritual life. And they did their work under most difficult conditions, at great sacrifice and with sincere devotion, which makes their accomplishments shine the more.[77]

This second period of Franciscan writing is also practical in the best sense of the word. It is not the literature of idle, learned monks who lived cut off from the world in rich monasteries. Such literature provided spiritual nourishment for those who needed it most. It is precisely that ordinary democratic trait, the endeavor to be of use to the people and to lead them to something better, which is to be found in all the literary activity of the Franciscans, from Divković to Jukić. It is one of its most beautiful qualities and at the same time one of its greatest merits.

5   The Serbian Orthodox Church: Its Evolution Under the Turks and Activity as a Distillation of Spiritual Life Among the Orthodox

Church Organization

An outline of what is known about the status of the Serbian Orthodox church and its development during Bosnia's independence can only be partial and nebulous.* Scarcely more is known, for that matter, about this church in Bosnia under the Turks, especially during the first century of their rule.

In the mid-fifteenth century even the shadow of Serbian national independence passed from the scene as the Turkish wave pressed into Syrmia [Srem] and Bosnia. At that point the patriarchate of Peć, upon which the Orthodox church in Bosnia depended, dropped out of sight too. All Orthodox centers came under the jurisdiction of the archbishop of Ohrid. Not until 1557 was the patriarchate reinstated, by Mehmed-Paša Sokolović. This most important grand vizier of the Turkish empire was the son of Orthodox parents from Bosnia. Brought as a child under the Adžami-Oglan[1] to Constantinople, Sokolović converted to Islam and subsequently gained power and enormous prestige.[2]

It is symptomatic of the relations between church and politics in those times that Mehmed-Pasha, even as vizier of the Turkish empire, did not once break connections with his nearest relatives who had remained loyal to Christianity. With the appointment of his brother Makarije as patriarch of Peć, he called the institution back to life in 1557.[3] Possibly he found its restoration expedient in consolidating the country. Possibly he was moved to help relatives rise to reputable positions. He named as bishop of Hercegovina his nephew Antonije

---

*See chapter 1.

and the latter, after Makarije's death in 1573, succeeded him as patriarch.

At approximately the time of the patriarchate's revival we find the earliest reference to a metropolitan of Zvornik.[4] That was the third such archbishopric in Bosnia. The invading Turks had encountered two centers: Dabar, whose seat was in the monastery of Banja, and Mileševo in Hercegovina, with its seat in the town of that name. All three bishoprics survived the vicissitudes of Turkish times, changing only residences and names, until they established themselves for good in the eventual administrative and trade centers, the bishopric of Dabar in Sarajevo (from 1713), that of Mileševo in Mostar (from 1766) and, finally, that of Zvornik in Tuzla (1852).[5]

Living Conditions

We can reconstruct in detail the Catholic clergy's life in Bosnia under the Turks. There are the monastery chronicles; the protocols of the Franciscan province; and especially the reports by official "visitors" and bishops, which were placed in the archives of the Congregatio de Propaganda Fide. But only meager information has come down to us concerning the activities and lives of the Serbian Orthodox clergy.

Judging by the few descriptions we have from occasional travelers who visited Bosnia and Serbia during that period, it would seem that the situation of the clergy was hard indeed. Georgijević, mentioned earlier, wrote that Orthodox priests lived in dire poverty in Serbia, reduced to selling firewood in the towns simply to survive.[6] This is confirmed by Gerlach in his travelogue of 1573: the clergy, without income, eked out a miserable existence unbecoming their station.[7] They wore the same clothing as simple peasants. Gerlach himself saw a priest conducting a funeral "barelegged to the knees."[8] The Frenchman Lefevre, who stayed in Mileševo in the year 1611, wrote that he encountered priests walking about half naked and so thin that they aroused the pity of all who saw them.[9]

Even in the nineteenth century Vuk Karadžić noticed that the Orthodox clergy wore "whatever they wanted"; that they "dug the earth, ploughed the land, cut the hay, chopped the wood"; and that they read the liturgy—many of them—"only once a year."[10]

As the eighteenth century wore on the position of these priests had changed for the worse in many respects. In 1767 the patriarchate of Peć was dissolved and Bosnia came under the immediate oversight of the patriarch of Constantinople. The consequences of this transfer were catastrophic for the development of the Serbian Orthodox church in Bosnia.

Greek Patriarchs

The dignity of ecumenical patriarch was obtainable through a firman of the sultan and it became a position, therefore, that was the object of open litigation. All the Greeks of Constantinople took a lively part, investing capital in this office just like any other business for profit.[11] The series of Greek bishops who left a legacy of "evil memories" dates to this time in Bosnia.[12] Just as they had obtained their offices, so they used these offices, brazenly and ruthlessly exploiting the clergy subordinate to them.[13]

And just as in Serbia, so in Bosnia these bishops were held to be a "scourge on the population." Alien in language and spirit, considering their ecclesiastical office to be strictly a profit center, they contributed nothing whatever to the spiritual and intellectual advancement of the dioceses entrusted to them. Quite the contrary, they worked manifold damage both materially and spiritually, often acting hand in glove with the Turks to the detriment of Christians.[14] From 1766 to 1880— the very century that was so rich in new ideas and cultural stimulation—they allowed the priesthood to remain needy at all times and on an inferior level of education. The Orthodox clergy's failure to develop literary skills, indeed its lack of any notable cultural accomplishment under Turkish hegemony, was largely attributable to the baneful work of these Greek bishops.

Greek bishops may have been a burden unique to the priesthood. But it need hardly be added that the clergy also labored under all the other disabilities shared generally by the suppressed *rayah*, burdens which were essentially the same for every non-Muslim. The nine-

teenth century saw Russia take the field against the Turks; it saw the
Serbs embark on open revolt; it saw the Montenegrins rise up in arms.
And this too was the century that saw the brunt of Turkish fury
descend on the Orthodox and their priests. For in them the Turks
detected the natural allies of their rebels, brethren in faith of the ones
leading the battle.

If now we recall that the Serbian Orthodox church centered on the
ecumenical patriarchate, which in turn centered on the Turkish empire, and that up to the eighteenth century the church enjoyed prac-
tically no support beyond the borders of that empire, then it becomes
abundantly clear why church life displayed the most primitive of
forms and church literature served purely the church's own most
parochial of needs.

Church Books

Serbian printing presses lasted only a short time;[15] the earliest decades
of Turkish rule saw an end to them. The first, founded in 1493 in Obod
by Đurađ Crnojević, soon shut down.[16] Nevertheless its imprints, few
though they were, found their way to monasteries in Hercegovina.[17]
The press at Goražde held out very little longer and of its work only a
prayer book (*euchologion*) and a psalter have survived. The latter, preserved in the Goražda Orthodox Church, says that it was printed
under the supervision of "hoary old father" Božidar Goraždanin by
the "pious monk and priest" Theodor in the year 1529.[18]

In the churches of Bosnia and Hercegovina are imprints, somewhat more numerous, issued by the press founded in Venice by
Božidar Vuković in 1520. Up until the middle of the 1500s his work was
continued by a son, Vinzenz, and in the latter half of the century
Orthodox church books were still being printed in Venice by one
Hieronymus Zagurović, a "patrician of Cattaro." He was supported by
a certain Jakob Krajkov from Sofia, while an individual named Kara-
Trifun saw to the sale of their books in Skoplje. In the Orthodox
churches of Čajnica and Travnik there are two psalters that came from
the Zagurović press.[19]

Also in the middle of the sixteenth century a printing press operated for a short while in Belgrad [sic][20] where its founder, Radiša Dimitrović, began printing a gospel. This work, interrupted by his death, was continued by Trojan Gundulić from Dubrovnik with the help of a monk, Mardarije, from Mrkšina Crkva. The resulting "Belgrade Gospel" can be found in two copies in the Hercegovinian monastery of Žitomislić.[21] In the same cloister can be found traces of activity on the part of Serbian printers in Romania. These people had been brought to Romania at the beginning of the next century, the seventeenth, at the behest of the Wallachian voivode Matthäus Bassarab, a kind of Maecenas to the Orthodox.[22]

Over their entire span of existence, at no time could the presses listed cover the demand for church books. The printing process was extremely slow, so books had to be copied by hand even when the presses were working. And after they disappeared *hand copying* was the only means of reproducing books like these. Such was the practice into the eighteenth century, to the moment when Russia began supplying the Serbian Orthodox churches with the books they needed. That explains why the surviving Bosnian Orthodox church books dating from those times consist more of manuscript copies than of imprints.[23]

For the most part they are service books in the narrowest sense of the word: psalters, canticles (*Cantuale*), rituals, gospels, and the like. With real literature such mechanical copying has nothing in common. Only rarely, moreover, is its artistic embellishment rich and tasteful. And yet these church books, with notes both by their copyists and by those who used them later, upon closer inspection offer many interesting data for judging the cultural conditions of the times, especially with respect to the impact of Turkish rule on the *rayah* and their church life.

Take, for instance, the *Paterikon* (teachings of the holy fathers), which has been kept in the museum of the church in Sarajevo since 1565. Its copyist noted that in those days of "need and sorrow" there were yet men among the townspeople who, while belonging to no monastery, looked after the church's religious and cultural needs.[24] Or take those standing formulas with which the copyists regularly closed their work, typically begging that any errors be forgiven and that the reader kindly not curse the copyist—they are not always just cut and dried, routine additions (as Prohaska believes), totally devoid of any real content. Some notes reflect church conditions, others the social or political environment, and off and on a few even provide information about the personal fate of the copyist.[25] Since there were few such copyists, since copying was a long, laborious job, and since to acquire books from abroad meant still more difficulty, cost, and risk, these transcribed books were treasured far beyond the ordinary and represented something of great value. That very same value was one reason why the Turks (and likely the occasional Christian as well), undeterred by the curse formulas normally pronounced at the ends of such books, pilfered and then resold them.[26]

As a rule the chronological entries refer to contemporary political events, changes of governors, changes on the throne, wars, natural phenomena, visits by bishops and patriarchs, or their deaths.

Even before the eighteenth century the monasteries in Bosnia were getting their church books from Russia. At Žitomislić there are some dating to 1637.[27] A steady influx of church books from that particular outside source, though, starts only in the next century. And the books thus acquired served purely church needs, narrowly defined.

Such a continuous rise in the use of Russian books in the Serbian Orthodox church resulted in the growing naturalization of the Russian language, and not merely within the church but in writing generally. Only with the coming of Vuk Karadžić and his epoch-making work did the vigor of Russian as an influence begin to slacken and wane toward its eventual elimination.

Literature

The nineteenth century saw the beginnings of literary activity among Bosnia's Orthodox population.[28] Archimandrite Joanikije Pamučina (1810–70) contributed to the *Srbsko-dalmatinski Magazin* and also collected folk tales. The monk Prokopije Čokorilo (1802–66), better known for his chronicle, attempted a dictionary of Turkish expressions in Serbo-Croatian. He likewise wrote for the *Srbsko-Dalmatinski Maga-*

zin and, through the good offices of Alexander Hilferding, contributed to various Russian publications. Apart from these men, a secular writer emerged for the first time, Ato Marković Šolaja.

Those early attempts are of interest because they made their appearance in Mostar. It was in Mostar that a literary center was to arise in the second half of the nineteenth century, which enriched Serbo-Croatian literature with such important poets and prose writers as Jovan Dučić, Aleksa Šantić, and Svetozar Ćorović.

Schools

Much more productive was the activity of the Orthodox church parishes themselves, as they went about founding and maintaining schools.

In this matter of schooling the Orthodox element showed greater understanding and achieved better results than the Catholic. That is because school concerns were not left solely in the hands of the clergy, as with the Catholics, but were the business of church congregations as well. And the latter consisted of laymen. (Afterwards they came to be known as "church and school parishes.") Here the townsfolk, who were tradespeople, for the most part, took an active role, influencing the direction of church activity and the appointment of clergy. These merchants, quite often widely traveled and worldly, doubtless were the stimulus behind the Orthodox schools in Bosnia. Also, being largely well-to-do, they provided the material wherewithal to establish them.

It is difficult to pin down just when the first such schools were established. According to the protocol of the Orthodox church in Sarajevo a certain Nikola Daskal ("teacher") was in residence there by 1682.[29] Jukić, surveying the school situation in Bosnia, expresses himself in vague generalities: in 1850 (he writes) the Serbian Orthodox population had had schools in all the larger settlements "for many years"; only the essentials were covered; and he cites eleven such towns.[30] The majority of these schools, it appears, were founded between 1820 and 1830.[31] Official data of the Turkish administration, on the other hand—data which can hardly be relied upon—tell us that Bosnia and Hercegovina together had fifty-seven Orthodox schools in 1870 with 2,820 male and 464 female pupils.[32]

In 1850 the first middle school was organized in Sarajevo on the basis of contributions and gifts from the Orthodox merchants. It represented a hybrid—part commercial and part classical—high school.[33] In 1866 the first Serbian Orthodox school of theology was founded in Banja Luka. Among the appointments to the teaching staff was Vasa Pelagić, well-known as a writer in the popular style with socialist tendencies. By 1869, however, Pelagić had been exiled to Asia on grounds (among other charges) that he taught gymnastics. For the Turks, gymnastics seemed to "bear a resemblance to military exercises."[34]

Monasteries

The Serbian Orthodox monasteries were of great importance, not only for the church but for the life of the people as a whole. Throughout the centuries of Turkish rule they constituted a kind of storage battery of popular energy, and monks enjoyed the people's sympathy and respect far more than did the secular clergy.[35]

In times of peace monasteries were centers of spiritual and intellectual life [des Geisteslebens]; in times of rebellion monks shared the fate of their people and often were its leaders.[36]

In Turkish times, however, the Serbian Orthodox church in Bosnia could not direct its energies outward; it generated no literary works comparable to those of the Franciscans. Conditions were extraordinary, and as a consequence this church confined its religious works to a minute number of meager forms. But behind them lay concealed a deep, intense life tightly wrapped within the most characteristic racial attributes and popular customs. This spiritual and intellectual life drew its strength from folk song, as well as from church books. It was rooted as deeply in the hearth of the peasant's hut as it was planted on the altar of the church.[37]

If, therefore, it is to the credit of the Catholic church and its representatives, the Franciscans, that a permanent link was maintained with the European West under Turkish hegemony, the merit and significance of the Orthodox church lay in its nursing the vital energies of the people as a whole and thus preserving the continuity of spiritual life and the unbroken national tradition into modern times.

Supplement The Hybrid Literature of the Bosnian Muslims as an Articulation of Islam's Effect on This Part of the Population

The part of Bosnia's population assimilating to Islam, which constituted a dominant warrior caste throughout Turkish rule, first directed its energies to conquest and then to the defense of property. This was a caste whose spiritual and intellectual life grew petrified in the twin molds of a foreign religion and an alien language.

Any literary activity pursued by individual Muslims from Bosnia took place by and large outside the country, in Constantinople, and in Turkish. (Or Arabic or Persian, as the case might be.) Turkish, to the majority of their cobelievers in Bosnia, was obscure at best or else totally unfamiliar. The writing of these expatriate Bosnian Muslims has no place in the present discussion, however meaningful or even meritorious it may have been. For it belonged to another culture entirely.[1]

Yet there is one area of spiritual-intellectual pursuit, limited though it was, which we cannot simply pass over in silence and still make any claim to complete coverage. We refer to efforts by the Muslims of Bosnia to create an art poetry in the seventeenth, eighteenth, and nineteenth centuries that made use of Arabic script.

The first person to take note of the existence of this kind of poetry was the historian and Russian consul in Bosnia, Alexander Hilferding.[2] The first, however, to treat the phenomenon of a hybrid literature in Bosnia scientifically, collecting and publishing all known manuscripts with proper understanding, was a certain Otto Blau who lived in Sarajevo as Prussian consul for a number of years (1861–72).[3] Not until 1912 did there appear a definitive critical edition of these Muslim poems.[4]

They are meager in quantity as well as low in quality: seventeen poems by eleven poets. Nonetheless, they deserve some attention as an interesting phenomenon of hybrid literature and a concrete example of the influence of oriental culture on Slavs.

Bosnians of Islamic faith did indeed retain their mother tongue. But from sheer necessity they took over a certain number of Turkish and Arabic expressions in consequence of Islam's administrative and, still more, religious institutions. The majority of Turkicisms introduced into the Serbo-Croatian spoken by Muslims are terms referring to the moral and religious concepts of Islam.

The Koran, cornerstone of Islam, may not be translated. Nevertheless it must be read by all schoolchildren and learned by heart, even if not always understood. In this way the Bosnian Muslims, by virtue of their religious instruction, simultaneously became conversant with the Arabic alphabet. Turkish itself, on the contrary, remained alien and unknown to the majority, for all that a certain number of Turkish expressions penetrated the language of the Muslim population. (Instruction in the religious schools—the *Mektefs*—was strictly limited to the alphabet and memorizing the Koran.)

The clergy, if they were to have any sort of pedagogical effect on the broadest popular strata in the spirit of Islam, were driven to using Serbo-Croatian. On religious grounds, however, they employed the Arabic alphabet—religious grounds, that is, plus lack of instruction in their own language and its written characters. Thus came into being Bosnia's hybrid verse.

In content the poems are largely didactic and religious. Most are composed in the form of *kasida* and *ilahija,* two species much favored in Turkish poetry of this tendency. The stanza consists of four trochaic lines of seven syllables apiece (rarely, eight), of which the first three rhyme and the fourth represents a refrain line. Turkish expressions abound, of course. Serbo-Croatian, to the extent it comes into play at all, is deformed and squeezed into a foreign poetic mold. The rhyme is nearly always false and irregular, the tone throughout arid and usually shallow.

Such poems were learned by heart, essentially, and a few of them, as for instance the didactic poem "Avdija," achieved great popularity among the Muslim population. Copies still extant deviate considerably from each other in form and content. It could not have been otherwise, considering that they were penned in an alphabet with no letter symbols for vowels. Thus the door was opened wide to mistakes in spelling and uncertainties in meaning.

In this area as well, the influence of Islam proved to be utterly restrictive and barren.

Notes

Abbreviations

MH   Monumenta Spectantia Historiam Slavorum Meridionalium (Zagreb, 1868–)

GZM   Glasnik Zemaljskog Muzeja u Bosni i Hercegovini (Sarajevo, 1889–)

JAZU   Jugoslavenske Akademije Znanosti i Umjetnosti

Introduction

1. Miroslav Karaulac, *Rani Andrić* (Belgrade: Prosveta, 1980).
2. Milorad Živančević, "Ivo Andrić u Poljskoj," Летопис Матице српске (Novi Sad, 1962) IV: 362–63.
3. Rastislav Drljić, "Pabirci o životu i radu Ive Andrića," *Dobri pastir* (Sarajevo, 1962) 11–12: I–IV, 376.
4. Dragoljub Vlatković, "Iz diplomatskog službovanja Ive Andrića," *Zbornik Matice srpske za književnost i jezik* (Belgrade, 1975) XXIII: 2, 385.
5. Vladislav Budisavljević Ministarstvu spoljnih poslova, Graz, 31 December 1923. (Documents in possession of Želimir B. Juričić; subsequent documents in the possession of Juričić are identified by his initials only.)
6. Budisavljević to Ninčić, Graz, 5 January 1924. (ŽBJ)
7. Budisavljević to Ninčić, Graz, 30 January 1924. (ŽBJ)
8. Andrić Ministarstvu spoljnih poslova, političko odeljenje, Graz, 11 February 1924. (ŽBJ)
9. Rešenje Ministra inostranih dela, Pr. Pov. Br. 681, Belgrade, 26 February 1924. (ŽBJ)

10. Quoted in Kosta Dimitrijević, *Razgovori i ćutanja Ive Andrića* (Belgrade: Kultura, 1976), 92.
11. Midhat Šamić, "Doktorat Ive Andrića," *Prilozi za književnost, jezik, istoriju i folklor* (Belgrade, 1975) XLI: 3–4, 261.
12. Karaulac, *Rani Andrić*, 136.
13. Drljić, "Pabirci o životu i radu Ive Andrića," 377.
14. Šamić, "Doktorat Ive Andrića," 265.
15. Želimir B. Juričić, ed. and trans., *Ivo Andrić: Letters* (Toronto: Serbian Heritage Academy, 1984), 96.
16. Ljubo Jandrić, *Sa Ivom Andrićem 1968–1975* (Belgrade: Srpska Književna Zadruga, 1977), 296.
17. The first Serbo-Croatian translation of Andrić's thesis appeared in 1982. For details, see Zoran Konstantinović, ed. and trans., *Andrić, Ivo: Razvoj duhovnog života u Bosni pod uticajem turske vladavine*, in *Sveske* (Belgrade: Zadužbina Ive Andrića, 1982) I, no. 1: 6–149.

1. Prologue: Spiritual Life in Bosnia Before the Turkish Conquest

1. Moriz Hoernes, "Alterthümer der Hercegovina" (Vienna, 1881 and 1882); *Dinarische Wanderungen* (Vienna, 1888).
2. "This inner poverty likewise testifies to the dreary spiritual emptiness of that generation which surrendered the faith of its forefathers as the price of its hunting grounds, stables and arsenals" (Hoernes, *Dinarische Wanderungen*, 342).
3. Vid Vuletić-Vukasović, *Bilježke o kulturi južnih Slavena, osobito Srbalja* (Dubrovnik, 1899).
4. Compare Petar Kaer, in *Prosvjeta* (Zagreb, 1895), 27.
5. Johann von Asbóth, *Bosnien und die Herzegovina* (Vienna, 1888).
6. Ibid., 106.
7. "The topography of Bosnia and Hercegovina is somewhere between those landforms that protect a country from overpowering outside influences (cf. Montenegro) and the other extreme that surrenders it helplessly to such influences" (Hoernes, *Dinarische Wanderungen*, 332).
8. Compare Ćiro Truhelka, "Tursko-slovjenski spomenici dubrovačke arhive," *GZM* XXIII (Sarajevo, 1911): 1ff. [*sic*].
9. Ćiro Truhelka, "Bosanska vlastela srednjeg vijeka," *Nada* (Sarajevo, 1901): 338.
10. Compare Franz Miklošić, ed., *Monumenta Serbica spectantia historiam Serbiae Bosnae Ragusii* (Vienna, 1858), 557.

11. Truhelka, "Tursko-slovjenski spomenici," 325. See also Konstantin Jireček, "Staat und Gesellschaft im mittelalterlichen Serbien," part 2, *Denkschriften der Kaiserlichen Akademie der Wissenschaften. Philosophisch-Historische Klasse* LVI, no. 3 (Vienna, 1912): 58ff.

12. What is at issue is the "Episcopatus Bestoensis" situated in Bistue (Šuica) at Duvanjsko polje in Hercegovina, or near modern Zenica in central Bosnia. Its bishop, Andreas, cosigned the acts of the First Council of Salona, so-called (A.D. 530), which were inserted in the manuscript of the *Historia Salonitana of Archdeacon Thomas* (ed., Franjo Rački, in *Scriptores*, vol. 3 of *MH*, vol. XXVI [Zagreb, 1894], see p. 18). Regarding authenticity, compare the recent work by Don Fr. Bulić and J. Bervaldi, "Kronotaksa solinskih biskupa, uz dodatok," a contribution to the *Bulletino di archeologia e storia dalmata* XXXV (Zagreb, 1912–13): 47ff.; page 51 has notes on the siting of the Bistue bishopric and the other suffragan bishoprics of Salona that overlapped Bosnian territory. See also Julian Jelenić, *Kultura i Bosanski Franjevci*, vol. I (Sarajevo, 1912), 15.

13. See the charter of Pope Alexander II (18 March 1067) in Franjo Rački, ed., *Documenta Historiae Chroaticae Periodum Antiquam [sic] illustrantia, MH*, vol. VII (Zagreb, 1877): 201–2; Philipp Jaffé, Samuel Loewenfeld, et al., *Regesta pontificum romanorum*, I: 4628; see also Jireček, "Staat und Gesellschaft," no. 3: 53 (1912); lastly, Alois Hudal, *Die serbisch-orthodoxe Nationalkirche* (Graz and Leipzig: U. Moser, 1922), 6, 9ff.

14. See P. Eusebius Fermendžin, "Acta Bosnae potissimum ecclesiastica," *MH* XXIII, no. 24 (Zagreb, 1892): 4.

15. Ibid., no. 74: 13. The papal legates stood helplessly by as the Patarins spread ever more widely. Thereupon, in 1246 Archbishop Benedict of Kalocsa at the head of his troops invaded Bosnia. The cross had been sent to him there by the pope, together with authorization to take the lands seized during the war from the Patarins and divide them among his soldiers, and then to incorporate the Bosnian bishopric into his own church province (Augustin Theiner, *Vetera monumenta historica Hungariam sacram illustrantia* I [Rome, 1859]: 373–74).

16. Vjekoslav Klaić, *Poviest Bosne do propasti kraljevstva* (Zagreb, 1882), 124; Jireček, "Staat und Gesellschaft," no. 3: 59.

17. Klaić, *Poviest*, 122–23. But see also Ludwig von Thallóczy, *Studien zur Geschichte Bosniens und Serbiens im Mittelalter*, trans. Franz Eckhart (Munich and Leipzig, 1914), 61ff.

18. So King Tvrtko II was characterized in 1435 by an Italian Franciscan. Compare Aegidius Carlerius, "Liber de legationibus," in *Monumenta Conciliorum Generalium seculi decimi quinti, Concilium Basileense, Scriptorum tomus primus* (Vienna, 1857), 676; see also Tvrtko II's self-defense in his letter to

Pope Martin V: "Quidam sui (of the king) emuli labia detractionis apperiunt, asserentes ipsum pro eo, quod infidelium et scismaticorum huius modi rex est, eos in ipsorum errore confovere. Cum tamen sanctae Romanae ecclesiae obediens et fidei catholicae cultor et augmentator existat. [Certain people who are jealous of him (of the king) open their lips in detraction asserting that because he is a king over infidels and schismatics of this kind he encourages them in their error. Yet he is nonetheless manifestly obedient to the holy Roman church, one who keeps the Catholic faith and increases it.] (Thallóczy, *Studien zur Geschichte*, 142).

19. Already at the beginning of the thirteenth century Ban Koloman, a son of the Hungarian king Andreas, surrendered Ponsa [Đakovo] to the Bosnian bishop as his domain (compare Klaić, *Poviest*, 124).

20. Klaić, *Poviest*, 345.

21. Theiner, *Vetera monumenta*, II: 235.

22. Klaić, *Poviest*, 289.

23. Ibid., 268.

24. Franjo Rački, "Bogomili i Patareni," *Rad JAZU* VIII (Zagreb, 1869): 152.

25. "Chronicon breve regni Croatiae Joannis Tomasich, minoritae ad annum," in Ivan Kukuljević-Sakcinski, ed., *Arhiv za povjestnicu jugoslovensku* IX (Zagreb, 1868): 17.

26. "The father rejected this in order not to call down upon himself the wrath of the Turks, for he was a new Christian and also had not driven the Manicheans from his land. I, on the other hand . . ." (Rački, "Bogomili i Patareni," VIII: 168–70).

27. "Kralj Srbljem, Bosni, Primorju, Humsci zemlji, Dalmaciji, Hrvatom, Donjim krajem, Zapadnim stranam, Usori, Soli, Podrinju, i k tomu."

28. Compare Fra Mijo Vjenceslav Batinić, *Djelovanje Franjevaca u Bosni i Hercegovini za prvih šest viekova njihova boravka* (Zagreb, 1881–87), I: 54.

29. Dragutin Prohaska, *Das kroatisch-serbische Schrifttum in Bosnien und der Herzegovina* (Zagreb, 1911), 29.

30. Augustin Theiner, *Vetera monumenta Slavorum Meridionalium historiam illustrantia* I (Rome, 1863): 19.

31. Janko Šafarik, "Srpski istorijski Spomenici Mletačkog arhiva," *Glasnik Srbskog Učenog Društva* XI (Belgrade, 1858 [*sic*]): 412–16.

32. Rački, "Bogomili i Patareni," VIII: 168.

33. Theiner, *Vetera monumenta Slavorum Meridionalium*, I: 12–13.

34. Klaić, *Poviest*, 346.

35. ". . . atque Chulmiae rex coronatus" in Ilarion Ruvarac, *O humskim episkopima i hercegovačkim metropolitima do godine 1766* (Mostar, 1901), 9.

36. Ibid.

37. Hudal, *Nationalkirche*, 56. See also Jireček, "Staat und Gesellschaft," IV

(*Denkschriften* LIV [*sic*; the correct vol. is LVI.—Eds.]), no. 2 (Vienna, 1919 [*sic*; the correct date is 1912—Eds.]): 49.

38. The statements that follow are based on Franjo Rački's fundamental research, "Bogomili i Patareni," in *Rad JAZU* VII (1868) [*sic*]: 84ff.; VIII (1869): 121ff.; and X (1870): 160ff. Concerning the newer literature on the question of the Bogomils see the extensive bilbiography by Miloš Weingart for his lecture "Počátky bogomilství," *Slovanský Přehled* XVI (Prague, 1913–14): 6ff.

39. Franjo Rački, "Prilozi za povjest bosanskih Patarena," *Starine* I (Zagreb, 1869): 138–40.

40. М. Г. Попруженко, ed., "Св. Козмы Пресвцтера Слово на Еретики," Памятники древней письменности и искусства CLXVII (St. Petersburg: 1907), [n.p.].

41. Compare Dragutin Ilijć [*sic*], "Srpska demokratija u srednjem veku," *Letopis Matice srpske* (1890): 163–64; and Prohaska, *Schrifttum*, 18.

42. Klaić, *Poviest*, 197.

43. Medo Pucić, *Spomenici srpski od 1395 do 1423* (Belgrade, 1858), 56.

44. Rački, "Bogomili i Patareni," VII: 229 [*sic*].

45. Klaić, *Poviest*, 243.

46. Compare Stojan Novaković, "Burkard i Bertrandon de-la-Brokijer," *Godišnjica Nikole Čupića* XIV (Belgrade, 1894): 44. This "gentleman . . . from Bosnia" was in all likelihood Radivoj, son of Stefan Ostoja, who repeatedly brought the Turks into Bosnia against King Tvrtko II Tvrtković, who converted to Catholicism under Stjepan Tomaš and who built a number of churches "as a sign of repentance for the grave sin he had committed in having previously brought the Turkish plunderers into his homeland" (compare Klaić, *Poviest*, 299).

47. Pucić, *Spomenici*, 28.

48. Georgii Fejér, *Codex diplomaticus* X, no. 5 (Buda, 1829–35 [*sic*]): 184.

49. Compare Ranke's remark: "Not even those Serbs and Bosnians, however, who preferred to subjugate themselves to the Turks, had any idea what they were doing, what fate held in store for them under their dominion" (Leopold von Ranke, *Serbien und die Türkei in XIX Jahrhundert*), in *Collected Works*, vols. 43 and 44 (Leipzig, 1879), 19.

50. Ranke, *Serbien und die Türkei*, 19.

51. Rački, "Bogomili i Patareni," X: 261.

52. According to the narrative of a contemporary, Gobellinus. See Rački, "Bogomili i Patareni," VIII: 168.

53. Truhelka, "Bosanska vlastela," 236.

54. Stojan Novaković, *Srbi i Turci XIV i XV veka*, Izdanje Čupićeva Zadužbina XXXIII (Belgrade: Državna štamparija, 1893), 99.

2. The Spread of Islam as a Direct Effect of Turkish Rule

1. These passages, as generally all in this dissertation discussing the impact of Turkish rule, are not to be taken as criticism of Islamic culture as such but only of the consequences of its transfer into a country that was Christian and Slavic.

2. Ranke, *Serbien und die Türkei*, 13.

3. Prohaska supports this view: "The development of Bogomilism was unfortunately cut short just at the time when a social and popular movement could have first blossomed" (*Schrifttum*, 18).

4. Milan Prelog, *Povijest Bosne u doba osmanlijske vlade* (Sarajevo: Naklada J. Studničke i druga, n.d.), I: 37–38.

5. Truhelka, "Tursko-slovjenski spomenici," 1–62, 303–50, 437–84.

6. Folk tradition, in the song about the Kosovo battle of 1389, explains the collapse of the Serbian state as follows: "On the very eve of the battle Tsar Lazar received a letter from heaven informing him that he would overcome the Turks in the impending battle next day if he decided in favor of an *earthly kingdom*. If, on the contrary, he decided for the *kingdom of heaven* he would be defeated and killed." Lazar chose the latter, losing both battle and life (see Vuk Stef. Karadžić, *Srpske narodne pjesme*, 2d ed. [Belgrade, 1895], II: 286).

7. Prelog, *Povijest Bosne*, I: 37–38.

8. "The Bosnian loves nothing so much as the land and property on which he grew up" (Asbóth, *Bosnien und die Herzegovina*, 162).

9. Ćiro Truhelka, *Die geschichtliche Grundlage der bosnischen Agrarfrage* (Sarajevo, 1911), 27.

10. "Here he rests . . . on his own noble ground"; "By laying myself to rest on my own noble ground I came to salvation" (see Vatroslav Jagić, "Nekoliko riječi o bosanskim natpisima na stećcima," *GZM* I [Sarajevo, 1890]).

11. Prohaska draws the following conclusion from both the inscriptions and the size of the gravestones: "These tombstones also had a practical or legal significance, for at the same time they usually were boundary markets delimiting the property of the deceased's family" (*Schrifttum*, 53).

12. One of the commonest curse formulas connected with the bestowal of land runs as follows: "He who annuls this our writ, be he our descendent or be he of foreign stock, let him be accursed by the Father and the Son and the Holy Ghost, by the twelve Apostles and the seventy-seven elect and may he be a fellow of Judas Iscariot, guilty along with him for spilling

the blood of God, and may he be damned by all the creatures of heaven" (Truhelka, *Der bosnischen Agrarfrage*, 26).

13. A converted Bosnian who, according to tradition, had killed King Lajos [Ludwig, Louis] II of Hungary in the battle of Mohacs (in 1526) was asked by the sultan what he wanted as a reward. "Nothing but your seal," he replied, "and your promise that we will not have to come to Constantinople to be granted our land allocations [*timar*]" (see Safvet-beg Bašagić, *Kratka uputa u prošlost Bosne i Hercegovine (od god. 1463–1850)* [Sarajevo: Vlastita naklada, 1900], 29). The same motif occurs in the Muslim folk song "Džanan buljukbaša i Rakocija," in Kosta Hörmann's collection, *Muhamedanske narodne pjesme* (Sarajevo, 1888), I: 25. Even more indicative is the legend of Beg Kopčić of Duvno. When the sultan gave this beg, who had caught Prince Rakoczy alive, free choice of his reward, the beg asked him for the gift of as much *ground* as he could ride around in one day. In his greed for a big piece of property he rode so far and drove his horse so hard that it fell down dead on the ground before the circle was closed. Thereupon the beg threw a stone as hard and far as he could just to be able to call a bit more ground his very own (see Mehmed-beg Kapetanović-Ljubušak, *Narodno blago* [Sarajevo, 1887], 578, 6 [*sic*] [The discrepancy may be due to the author's having used a later edition, *Istočno Blago*, Sarajevo, 1896 and 1897.—Eds.].

14. Vjekoslav Klaić, *Bosna. Podatci o zemljopisu i poviesti Bosne i Hercegovine* (Zagreb, 1878), 90. By way of example the Bosnian begs on the eve of the Austro-Hungarian occupation gave the following answer to their Christian fellow countrymen, who foresaw property loss for the begs upon the entry of a Christian power: "Let the *giaour* (infidel) come, let him take over Bosnia! In that case I'll open my document box, I'll let myself be baptised, I'll eat pork and—stay just as I am, a beg, and you'll stay just what you were before, a Christian laborer. If the cross isn't that heavy for you it won't be for me either. If pig's meat doesn't stick in your throat, well, it won't stick in mine" (see Antun Knežević, "Kako se zemlje u Bosni diele," *Bosanski Prijatelj* IV [Zagreb, 1870]: 182).

15. Prelog, *Provijest Bosne*, II: 47.

16. Hörmann, *Narodne pjesme*, I: 401; Andrić's emphasis.

17. Petar Petrović Njegoš, *Gorski vijenac*, 8th ed. (Belgrade, 1923), 29.

18. Slavoljub Bošnjak [I. F. Jukić], *Zemljopis i poviestnica Bosne* (Zagreb: Berzotiskom narodne tiskarnice Ljudevita Gaja, 1851), 143.

19. See Franz Kidrič, *Bartolomaeus Georgijević*, vol. II of *Mitteilungen des Museion* (Vienna, 1920).

20. Milan Vukičević, *Srpski narod, crkva i sveštenstvo u turskom carstvu od 1459–1557 god.* (Belgrade, 1896), 15.

21. Čedomilj Mijatović, "Pre trista godina. Prilog k izučavanju izvora za istoriju našeg naroda u XVI-om veku," *Glasnik srpskog učenog društva* XXXVI (Belgrade, 1872): 190.
22. Ibid., 119.
23. Vukičević, *Srpski narod*, 17.
24. Ranke, *Serbien und die Türkei*, 529.
25. Truhelka, "Tursko-slovjenski spomenici," 181, [*sic*].
26. Prelog, *Povijest Bosne*, I: 48.
27. A traveler (G. Batt. Montealbano) remarked on the phenomenon in 1625 that "chi ha il fratello, chi il figliuolo, chi il padre et il parento Turco [One has a Turk for a brother, another a son, still another has Turks for father and kinsman]." See Ranke, *Serbien und die Türkei*, 525).

3. The Social and Administrative Institutions of Islam

1. As an example, in 1865 when the *Kanun* was rarely being applied, Mehmed Huršid Paša presented to the Sarajevo priest Fra Grgo Martić a little seal ring "with Martić's name inscribed in Arabic letters" (Jelenić, *Kultura i Bosanski Franjevci*, I: 295).
2. "Push them hard till they pay the poll tax and are humiliated," runs the Sura (passage) of the Koran that regulates relations between Muslims and other faiths. Compare the Bosnian Muslim proverb, "The *rayah* is like the grass, / Mow it as much as you will, still it springs up anew" (Kapetanović-Ljubušak, *Narodno blago*, 203).

   Njegoš voiced the same perspective in his song honoring Sultan Bajazid when he wrote,

   > Kada Bosni polomi rogove,
   > Kad sve pokla što ne posuneti,
   >   Samo fakir ostavi fukaru,
   > Da nam služi, a pred krstom tuži.

   (Once you'd broken Bosnia's horns / You mowed down what would not be pruned / Leaving only the riffraff behind / So there'd be someone left to serve us and grieve before the cross.) (Njegoš, *Gorski vijenac*, 45).
3. A contemporary Dominican, who himself had languished in Turkish captivity for more than twenty years, had this to say about the Bosnian Christians (1475–81): "Propter tributar annualia et onera gravia et multas incommoditates quas patiuntur, ita depauperati sunt, quod vix se nutrire

possunt" (*Libellus de ritu et moribus Turcorum* [Wittemberg: Iohann Lufft, 1530], VIII: 23). [Because of the annual tributes, heavy labor, and many inconveniences they suffer they are so pauperized that they can hardly feed themselves.] On the author and the time of this work's composition, to which Martin Luther provided a preface, see the printing of the latter in O. Clemen's critical edition of Luther's complete works in thirty volumes (Weimar, 1909), II: 198ff.

4. Jovan Cvijić, "Des migrations dans les pays Yougoslaves," *Revue des Études Slaves* III, nos. 1–2 (Paris, 1923): 5.

5. The fact had already been observed around 1530 by Benedikt Kuripešić and set down in his well-known travelogue: "Turks, as they travel here and there, take from Christians everything they have without paying for it, wherefore poor folk withdraw into the mountains to fertile elevations, conveying their goods thither and cultivating the ground" (see Petar Matković, "Putovanja po balkanskom poluotoku XVI vieka. II," *Rad JAZU* LVI [1881]: 175). So, for instance, the Franciscan monastery of Fojnica had to pull back into the mountains in the sixteenth century from the "beautiful valley along the highway . . . because it could no longer minister to uninvited guests" (Fra Mijo Vjenceslav Batinić, *Franjevački samostan u Fojnici od XIV–XX stoljeća* [Zagreb, 1913], 21). The monastery's new situation can best be seen in the account of the Franciscan papal visitor Paolo de Rovigno, who visited the place in 1640. He found it gloomy and sad (*"che rende malinconia grande"*) and felt as though he were in a prison there (*"quasi che in carcere"*) (see Stipan Zlatović, "Izvještaj o Bosni god. 1640 o. Pavla iz Rovinja," *Starine* XXIII [Zagreb, 1890]: 24).

6. "The Christian populace retreated as far as possible into the mountains, there to live their lives in their own way, with the result that they turned back to primitive economic forms and certain customs such as bride-stealing and blood revenge with which the Serbian state had struggled energetically" (Matthias Murko, *Das Serbische Geistesleben* [Leipzig and Munich: Süddeutsche Monatshefte, 1916], 8). With few exceptions, this general statement holds good for Bosnia as well.

7. Batinić, *Djelovanje franjevaca*, II: 36; and Lorenz Rigler, *Die Türkei und deren Bewohner* (Vienna, 1852), I: 186.

8. Jukić, *Zemljopis i poviestnica Bosne*, 143. In his study of guild organization in Skoplje (Üsküb), Veselinović claims that of the existing forty-two crafts organized into guilds, only twenty-five were accessible to Christians, "while 17 others were reserved exclusively for the Turks. . . . So far as I could ascertain, the Turks on political grounds did not admit Serbs, as generally any Christian, to apprenticeship in the manufacture of weapons and knives, and they were debarred from the other 15 crafts because

these seemed to the Turks easier and more profitable" V. M. [*sic*] Veselinović, "Esnafi u Skoplju," *Godišnjica Nikole Čupića* XV [Belgrade, 1895]: 232).

9.   "It is indeed sad that a man who, after six days of work, on the seventh ought to be devoting his heart and mind to God in quiet meditation is, on that very day, required to work the hardest" (Jukić, *Zemljopis i poviestnica Bosne*, 162).

10. Batinić, *Djelovanje franjevaca*, III: 215.

11. Of Ali-Paša Stočević, who during the first half of the nineteenth century was vizier and all but unlimited ruler of Hercegovina, his contemporary, the monk Prokopije Čokorilo, wrote that he "taxed the dead for six years after their demise" and that his tax collectors "ran their fingers over the bellies of pregnant women, saying 'you will probably have a boy, so you have to pay the poll tax right away'" (Vladimir Ćorović, "Iz dnevnika Prokopije Čokorila," *GZM* XXV [Sarajevo, 1913]: 103). The following folk saying from Bosnia well reveals how taxes were exacted: "He's as fat as if he'd been tax collecting in Bosnia."

12. Bašagić, *Kratka uputa*, 116. [Andrić refers to this work throughout as "Poviest Bosne."—Eds.]

13. The first part of this proclamation is indicative of Christian-Jew relations. It reads thus:

> With this letter we give notice to each Christian of the following command of our masters the Turks, insofar as they have shown us their grace and favor by entrusting us with communicating to each Christian in the church the following: First, that Christian men and women are not permitted to go on outings and may not sing during said outings, nor in their houses, nor in other places. Second, they are not to dress up nor wear jewelry nor stand dressed up like that before the doors of their houses. If a woman likes jewelry she should put it on at home and not wear it in public. Their daughters may not decorate themselves with ducats and if anyone is in a position to dress up a daughter, he should not let her go outdoors. Our masters like it not and so neither does God. Third, Brethren, our masters gave orders that all Christians walk humbly (submissively), crossing hands over breasts in front of all Turks to show that Turks are placed over us. Fourth, as we have repeatedly admonished you, Christians must not dress like Turks or janissaries, for our masters will not tolerate that. Those who do not obey will be severely punished—and do not say that we have not shared this with you. We all must

suffer because of the rashness of a few. Etc. (Vlad. Skarić, "Jedna naredba o rajinom odijelu iz doba otomanske vladavine," *GZM* XIV [1902]: 557).

14. Wives of Jews wore almost the same clothing as Muslims, only they were prohibited from wearing red or yellow boots. But it seems that Jewish women very often and very gladly violated this prohibition. Their preference for colored boots became a regular burden on the Jewish community, a fact that stands out clearly in the nineteenth-century *Pinakes*, where year in, year out we see repeated entries like the following:

> To the captain of the guard, for wearing yellow boots .. 2 groš,

> To the muteselim, to prevent his noticing the footwear
> of the women .... 3 groš,

and so on. (A *groš* was a Turkish coin worth about eight kreutzers.) (Moritz Levy, *Die Sephardim in Bosnien* [Sarajevo: Daniel A. Kajon, 1911], 55).

15. Johann Rośkiewicz, *Studien über Bosnien und die Hercegovina* (Leipzig and Vienna, 1868), 188–89.

16. Prelog, *Provijest Bosne*, II: 97.

17. Rośkiewicz, *Studien*, 251.

18. Martin Nedić, *Stanje Redodržave Bosne Srebrene poslje pada kraljevstva Bosanskog pak do okupacije* (Gjakovo, 1884), 52.

19. That was the Mehmed-Paša who "was unwilling to condemn the worst offenders to death but was content with a fine, and whose chief maxim was 'better to be a silversmith [*Silberschmied*] than a butcher'" (Batinić, *Djelovanje Franjevaca*, III: 119). [Original has *kujundžija* 'goldsmith'—Eds.]

20. Julian Jelenić, *Ljetopis franjevačkog samostana u Kreševu* (Sarajevo, 1918), 32–33. [Separate reprint of an article by the same title in *GZM* XXIX (1917).—Eds.]

21. "Protocullum Induit. Conv. Sutjescae," in Batinić, *Djelovanje Franjevaca*, II: 45. [Andrić and *Sveske* mistakenly have "251."—Ed.]

22. See *Starine* XXIII (1890), 32–33: "In questo convento i fratri sono come in carcere." Because of the frequent surprise attacks, the door of the monastery in Gradovrh was reinforced with iron ("Tutta fodrata di diverse sorte di ferro"). [Reference is to Stipan Zlatović, "Izvještaj o Bosni."—Ed.]

23. "Whoever has seen the rectory of Grabnica or any of the other Christian rectories in this land can draw his own conclusions as to the state of Hercegovina under Turkish rule. That rectory is so nervously perched on the edge of the stone wasteland, as if fearing to set foot inside the oasis of green. The doors are so low that one can only enter bent double, with the

object of keeping the Turks from penetrating the houses or chapels on horseback, as in their sacrilegious insolence they were in the habit of doing" (Hoernes, *Alterthümer*, 126).

24. Levy, *Sephardim*, 113.

25. Ibid., 116ff. It is characteristic of the Turkish administration that the vizier, just as he had for similar documents drawn up for Christians, used the formula affirming that "this synagogue existed before the conquest of Bosnia by the Osmanlis," even though the first Jews migrated into Bosnia only toward the middle of the sixteenth century.

26. See Batinić, *Franjevački samostan u Fojnici*, 35: "The silence of the cloister would be disturbed by the heathen hullabaloo of the Turks who would come in uninvited, eating and drinking and thieving and stealing whatever fell into their hands. The *musafirhana* (guesthouse for strangers) that the Franciscans had built near the monastery confronted them with such a dilemma that it is hard to describe the sacrifice and effort it cost or the worry and anxiety it involved, both night and day."

27. Kemura and Ćorović, "Prilozi za historiju pravoslavne crkve u Bosni i Hercegovini u xviii i xix stoljeću," *GZM* XXIV (1912): 436.

28. So, for instance, in the year 1780: "On 12 July the guardian was called to Travnik because the cursed kadi had reported him for wearing his cross at a burial service and before the proceedings were over we had to pay a fine of 1,300 groš." In 1781, again, 400 groš, and so on (Jelenić, *Ljetopis*, 80).

29. Vukičević, *Srpski narod*, 49. John Burbery, who as member of an embassy in 1664 traveled throughout the South Slavic lands, noted the following detail in Philippopolis [Plovdiv]: "In this settlement there is an old tower with a bell, which struck us as somewhat unusual because we had not seen a single bell up to that point in these barbaric regions" (in Stojan Novaković, "Putničke beleške o balkanskom poluostrvu XVII i XVIII veka," *Godišnjica Nikole Čupića* XVII [1897]: 87).

30. "Only in Sutjeska did the church preserve bells from earlier times. The largest weighed 100 pounds. One has the year 1595 imprinted upon it and from the inscription written there we see that it was cast in Ofen [Buda]. Bells were hung under the church roof. . . . The inhabitants of Vareš had a bell too, 50 pounds in weight, which they likewise had hung under the roof of the church. But that bell cost them dearly, for they paid more in money fines than the whole bell weighed to begin with" (Nedić, *Stanje Redodržave Bosne*, 57–58).

31. "This we were permitted, and the ringing of a bell was heard in Kreševo, the *first* in Bosnia with the exception of the quite insignificant little bell which was a holdover in Vareš from earlier times and the one in Jajce at

St. John's, two hours outside the town" (Fra Grgo Martić, *Zapamćenja* [Zagreb, 1906], 47).

32. Ibid.
33. Ibid.
34. Ibid., 82–83.
35. Batinić, *Franjevački samostan u Fojnici*, 105. Settling the dispute over the organ "and other, smaller, vexations" cost the monastery 7,516 groš, whereas its complete outlay for the whole year, including the brothers' food and clothing and so on, came to only 5,230 groš.
36. See note 13 above.
37. See Hoernes, *Dinarische Wanderungen*, 149, 230; and Rośkiewicz, *Studien*, 179, 262. Even a Turkish traveler, Evlija Čelebi, in a travel account in which he found everything in Bosnia to be thriving and well-ordered, could say of the roads only that they were "very bad" (Kemura, "Iz Sejahatname Evlije Celebije," *GZM* XX [1908]: 184).
38. "Roads in Bosnia are so constructed as to seem as if they had come into being of their own accord or as nature had created them." "They (the Turks) care not a whit about the building of roads and bridges, consequently it is an annual event that many travelers break their necks or drown in the floods" (Jukić, *Zemljopis i poviestnica Bosne*, 9, 154).
39. "Proh. dolor, post tot excruciatus, si adminus curarent vias quibus vehi possit" runs the comment apropos this by Petar Bakula in his chronicle. [Alas! the pain after having been tormented so many times, if only they'd attend to roads one could ride over!] (Hoernes, *Dinarische Wanderungen*, 63).
40. Martić, *Zapamćenja*, 50–51.
41. Bašagić, *Kratka uputa*, 159. When this same vizier ordered that the houses in Travnik be numbered, the Bosnian Muslims met even that harmless innovation with mistrust and scornfully dubbed Ćamil-Paša "Tahtar," or "Little Tablet Man," after the small wooden plaques on which the house numbers were written (ibid.).
42. Rośkiewicz, *Studien*, 424.
43. The extent of Bosnian isolation may be judged by these examples: Whereas during the kingdom the people of Bosnia, especially the nobility, at least kept up a lively commerce with Ragusa (see chapter 1), an old landed gentleman from Trebinje, a Muslim, confessed to Dr. Josef K. Koetschet in 1866 that he had never in his life been to Dubrovnik [Ragusa], though it was only a few hours away (*Osman Pascha* [Sarajevo, 1909], 12). Vuk Vrčević, speaking of the Bosnian Muslims, made the following observation: "Rare are those who have gotten to the seacoast, rare birds indeed who have traveled the world over [*weisse Raben*, 'white

ravens,' *rares aves*], while so far as I am aware not a single one has ever ventured upon the open sea" (*Narodne pripovjedke i presude* [Dubrovnik, 1890], 43). Compare also the Bosnian proverb, "No mountain ever comes higher than your own house's threshold" (Većeg brda od kućnog praga nema) (Kapetanović-Ljubušak, *Narodno blago*, I: 280, 28).

44. Compare Ljub. Stojanović, "Stare srpske štamparije," *Srpski Književni Glasnik* VII (1902): 456.

45. Jukić, *Zemljopis i poviestnica Bosne*, 157.

46. Ignacije Strukić, *Povjestničke crtice Kreševa i franjevačkog samostana* (Sarajevo, 1899), 121–22.

47. Hamdija Kreševljaković, *Kratak pregled hrvatske knjige u Herceg-Bosni* (Sarajevo, 1912), 26.

48. Levy, *Sephardim*, 31.

49. "The implements in use to this day among the country and small town populations—their ploughs, carts, mills, crockery, etc.—bring to mind a prehistoric tradition before ever they do a medieval one" (Hoernes, *Dinarische Wanderungen*, 334). And here is a traveler from the last years of Turkish hegemony describing Bosnia's economic conditions: "Animal stock there is aplenty but as for milk, butter, cheese—nothing of any value. Land there is on all sides, but no agriculture, no orchards, no vineyards. Bees there are in abundance, but no beekeepers. All crafts exist only in embryo, tools date from the time of Adam, and as for cartmakers, stonemasons, blacksmiths—hardly a trace" (Mihovil Pavlinović, *Puti* [Zadar, 1888], 100).

50. Jelenić, *Kultura i Bosanski Franjevci*, II: 211.

51. Ibid., II: 187.

52. Compare Bašagić, *Kratka uputa*, 40.

53. Compare Ćiro Truhelka, "Gazi Husrefbeg, njegov život i njegovo doba," *GZM* XXIV (Sarajevo, 1912): 91–232.

54. For instance, during Vizier Husrefbeg's invasion of Dalmatia around 1528 the booty was so considerable that a "simple Turkish soldier who to that moment had not had a penny to his name suddenly found himself the master of ten slaves" (Bašagić, *Kratka uputa*, 32).

55. Prelog, *Povijest Bosne*, I: 166.

56. Batinić, *Djelovanje Franjevaca*, III: 88.

57. "From earliest times the begs held all legal authority in their domains in their own hands and exercised it totally as autonomous lords without bothering about imperial firmans or viziers' ordinances. They themselves did the collecting of government taxes and the functionaries sent out by the vizier were sent right back to Travnik, either by the use of bribes or

the application of force, with trifling sums in their hands" (Bašagić, *Kratka uputa*, 63).

58. Compare Bašagić, *Kratka uputa*, 54; and Prelog, *Povijest Bosne*, 85. [Source found on p. 84—Eds.]

59. Bašagić, *Kratka uputa*, 82.

60. Ibid., 102.

61. Jelenić, *Kultura i Bosanski Franjevci*, II: 62.

62. Koetschet, *Osman Pascha*, 85.

63. Jelenić, *Kultura i Bosanski Franjevci*, II: 60.

64. "The viziers and their staff I'd say at first glance to be educated, progressive people, real Frenchmen, Prussians, etc. But look a little closer and there's nothing but the uniform" (Jukić, *Zemljopis i poviestnica Bosne*, 155).

65. Antun Knežević, *Carsko-turski namjestnici u Bosni i Hercegovini godine 1463–1878* (Zagreb, 1882 [*sic*]), n.p.

66. Martin Gjurgjević, *Memoari sa Balkana (1858–1878)* (Sarajevo, 1911), 320 [*sic*].

67. Viz., Kreševo and Fojnica; see notes 68 and 69 below.

68. Jelenić, *Ljetopis*, 28.

69. Here are just a few entries from the 1789 accounts kept by the Franciscan monastery in Fojnica:

> For the miserable, lousy fine .... 350.– groš
>
> To the vojvode, so he won't mistreat me in jail 4.5
>
> To Dinić, so he won't go to the kadi 3.4
>
> For the wine the Turks swiped from us (43 okas) 2.96
>
> Present for the kajmakam (district headman) 55.–
>
> Cost to the Kreševo monastery in 1873 of getting a
> firman in Constantinople 2171.–
>
> of which:
>
> > To Beglučki effendi .... 2000.–gr.
> >
> > And to his scribe, for running around and cheating
> > everywhere .... 100.–gr.

And so it goes (Batinić, *Franjevački samostan u Fojnici*, 94).

70. The chronicler of the Tvrdoš monastery near Trebinje noted the following in the year 1651: "During that period the monasteries suffered much want and misery: instead of aspers by the thousands being squeezed out

of them it was groschen by the three and four thousands" (240 aspers equalled 1 groš) (Ćorović, "Hercegovački manastiri: I. Trebinski manastir (Tvrdoš)," GZM XXIII [1911]: 510).

71.   "Acts of violence and extortion by the Pašas against the Jews plunged them into the depths of darkest night. . . . There were many unpleasant run-ins with the authorities from time to time, which, however, were susceptible of settlement by means of money" (Levy, Sephardim, 28, 35).

72.   Ibid., 43. (16 puli were the equivalent of 1 groš.) Christians too were subjected by the Turks to forced labor—on Sundays—as shown by the folk song in Vuk Stef Karadžić, Život i običaji naroda srpskog (Vienna, 1867), 205.

73.   Levy, Sephardim, 58–60. Loss on money exchange appears to have been a systematic extortion procedure that Turkish governors applied against Jews. Such items turn up regularly in the Pinakes over many years.

74.   For the sake of completeness it should be stressed that among the governors and the rest of Turkish officialdom there also appeared entirely correct and incorruptible men who had the well-being of the country at heart and were imbued with a feeling for justice—if only in the Islamic sense of the term. Apart from the Bosnians Gazi Husrefbeg (1506) and Grand Vizier Mehmed-Paša Sokolović (1564–79), whose public buildings even today testify to their efforts on behalf of and their interest in the general public, there were besides other righteous and noble-minded governors. Murtada-Paša (1623–26), also a Bosnian, as governor distributed a dowry to poor young women so that the Muslim population, which had shrunk, should multiply (see Bašagić, Kratka uputa, 62). Batinić writes that a special emissary of the sultan, Ali-aga, who was in Bosnia during 1773, was a man "eminently wise" who behaved justly toward Christians as toward Muslims and was absolutely incorruptible. (Offers of money he declined with the simple words, "I do not want this. I have been given more by my sultan than I need" (Batinić, Djelovanje Franjevaca, III: 136). The Franciscan Fra Bono Benić in his chronicle depicts Ali-Paša Hedžimović as "kind, clever, and in military matters sensible" (Nada [Sarajevo, 1895]: 265).

75.   See Karadžić, Život i običaji, 264.

76.   "The kadi's love of bribes has long passed into proverb and I am convinced that if some kadi had wanted to be original and not take bribes he would not have had any credibility with anyone" (Koetschet, Osman Pascha, 10). "Justice in Turkey was always for sale. In order to win a trial, even when provided with the best of material evidence, the gold on the scale of the judge had to be heavy" (Batinić, Djelovanje Franjevaca, III: 150).

77.   When the Turks first appeared at the beginning of the 1400s, the people

of Ragusa were writing that "they do nothing without a bribe" (Pucić, *Spomenici*, v.) De la Broquière, quoted earlier, said of the Turks under the year 1432 in his book of travels, "No one can even talk with them without bringing a present" (see in Novaković, "Burkard i Bertrandon de-la-Brokijer," XVIII: 43). [Correct reference is to volume XIV.—Eds.]

78. "Over the course of time they had so adapted themselves to the thought processes of their masters that they struck back with the same wea-pons—*cunning and craft*" (Prelog, *Povijest Bosne*, I: 52). "The Slavic type through intercourse with the Turks only acquired a predilection for laziness and carelessness, following their evil example" (Rigler, *Die Türkei und deren Bewohner*, I: 176). "It is noteworthy how often the Christians leave things up to Fate—something they have learned from the Turks" (Jukić, *Zemljopis i poviestnica Bosne*, 29).

79. "The yoke of fear has forced him into lying and gotten him used to insincerity, with the result that he tells lies often and without much reason. The yoke of fear, furthermore, has blunted the sense of commu-nity among the Bosnian Christians" (Klaić, *Bosna. Podatci o zemljopisu*, 103 [according to A. Hilferding—author's note]). Mihovil Pavlinović talks of a dearth of "cordiality and candor which was forced on even the best Bosnians over centuries of oppression and Asiatic wiliness" (*Puti*, 108).

80. F. S. Krauss and J. Duimo Beckmann, "Über den Einfluss des Orients auf die Südslaven," *Das Ausland* 15 (Stuttgart and Munich, 1887): 286.

4. The Spiritual and Intellectual Life of the Catholic Populace Under the Turks

1. Jelenić endorses this view in his *Kultura i Bosanski Franjevci* (I: 26–32), following Mark of Lissabon's "Chronica fratrum minorum." According to another opinion, which is shared by Batinić and the majority of the Bosnian Franciscans and was first advanced by Wadding, Franciscans were to be found in Bosnia by the first half of the thirteenth century establishing a Bosnian vicariate (Luca Hibernus Waddingus, *Annales Mi-norum seu Trium Ordinum a S. Francisco institutorum*, 2d ed. [Rome, 1731]). The view held by Jelenić appears to be more certain and better founded.

2. Batinić, *Djelovanje Franjevaca*, I: 126.

3. Jelenić, *Kultura i Bosanski Franjevci*, I: 92.

4. Batinić, *Djelovanje Franjevaca*, I: 125–26.

5. Daniele Farlati, *Illyrici sacri tomus quartus* (Venice, 1769): 74; compare

Rački, "Prilozi za zbirku srbskih i bosanskih listina," *Rad JAZU* I (Zagreb, 1867): 162.

6. Batinić, *Djelovanje Franjevaca,* I: 132.

7. The Chronicle of Fra Nikola Lašvanin reads as follows: "At the gathering of the Fratres Minores of St. Francis of Assisi the province of Bosnia was divided into Bosnia Argentina and Croatian Bosnia, for the Turks do not allow the Franciscans within their empire to be subject to those who are under another government" (Jelenić, *Kultura i Bosanski Franjevci,* I: 122).

8. Petar Bakula, *I Martirii nella Missione Francescana Osservante in Ercegovina* (Rome: Tisak Monaldi, 1862), 13ff.; Jelenić, *Kultura i Bosanski Franjevci,* I: 124–27.

9. See Karlo Horvat, "Monumenta historica nova historiam Bosnae et provinciarum vicinarum illustrantia," *GZM* XXI (1909): 393ff.

10. Bishop Fra Nikola Ogramić, in his capacity as confidential advisor to Emperor Leopold I, accompanied General Leslie on his Slavonian incursions (1684), and incited the Christians there to revolt. Meanwhile the Franciscan Luka Ibrišimović took part in the battles as leader of a group of volunteers and gained special distinction in the struggle against the Turks (see Batinić, *Djelovanje Franjevaca,* II: 160).

11. Donato Fabianich, *Firmani inediti dei Sultana di Constantinopoli* (Florence, 1884), 52–57.

12. Fra Mijo Vjenceslav Batinić, "Njekoliko priloga k bosanskoj crkvenoj poviesti," *Starine* XVII (Zagreb, 1885): 91–94.

13. Particularly burdensome was the tax known as the *Đulus,* which from the end of the seventeenth century the Franciscans had to pay to the imperial administrator for the right to perform church services freely. In a special ceremony the guardians of all the monasteries each year handed over to the vizier 1,300 groš in cash, a ram, several kilos of sugar, twelve loaves of bread, and as many bars of soap. The sum of 1,300 groš was considerable for the time. It meant that the monasteries, in order to put such an amount together, often had to borrow at high interest, especially since the viziers changed frequently and the Franciscans would often have to pay the *Đulus* thrice over in one and the same year (see Batinić, *Djelovanje Franjevaca,* III: 145).

14. I. Jastrebov, "Sadržaj fermana koje je izradilo sebi katoličko sveštenstvo kod porte o svom odnošaju prema pravoslavnom mitropolitu hercegovačkom i bosanskom," *Glasnik Srpskog Učenog Društva* XLVIII (Belgrade, 1880): 405ff.

15. Nedić, *Stanje Redodržave Bosne Srebrene,* 37.

16. Batinić, *Djelovanje Franjevaca,* II: 23, III: 111–12; and Jelenić, *Kultura i Bosanski Franjevci,* I: 191–94.

17. Batinić, *Djelovanje Franjevaca*, III: 182.
18. Ibid., III: 188ff.
19. Prohaska, *Schrifttum*, 85.
20. Radoslav Glavaš, *Život i rad fra Rafe Barišića* (Mostar, 1900); Jelenić, *Kultura i Bosanski Franjevci*, II: 22–73.
21. See Horvat, *Monumenta historica.* That the Bosnian Franciscans, even in purely religious matters, were subject to a certain amount of influence from conditions in their homeland can be seen from the example of Fran Juraj Dobretić. At the court of the Medici prince Lorenzo the Magnificent, Dobretić achieved great repute as a theologian and was much prized. Yet in the end he had to leave Italy, not only for defending Savonarola but for works that "reeked" of Patarin doctrine, "doctrine from which he could not liberate himself on account of his upbringing and the circumstances prevailing in his homeland" (Batinić, *Djelovanje Franjevaca*, II: 6–8).
22. Prohaska, *Schrifttum*, 39.
23. Batinić, *Djelovanje Franjevaca*, II: 17.
24. Right down to the last days of Turkish rule Franciscans very frequently dressed in the national costume or other worldly clothing, be it from necessity, habit, or preference. Fra Grgo Martić, poet and priest of Sarajevo, wore in and around 1860 a coat (as he himself wrote) "in European style such as no one in Bosnia has," with which he had been presented by a dragoman from one of the consulates (Martić, *Zapamćenja*, 17). The bishop of Mostar, Fra Anđeo Kraljević, accompanied by two servants, rode about in 1878 dressed as a Turk, "like a Kadi or a Mufti," only with this difference, that he wore a golden cross on his chest at the end of a heavy chain (Gjurgjević, *Memoari*, 170). That this privilege now and then was abused is evident from the fact that in 1765 the provincial, Fra Bono Benić, forbade the wearing of "pompous civilian clothes" and Bishop Fra Marian Dobretić in 1779 prohibited *"sub poena inabilitatis ad officia"* the wearing of gold-embroidered belts and weapons ("even if the gold be not genuine") (Jelenić, *Kultura i Bosanski Franjevci*, II: 146).
25. Jelenić, *Kultura i Bosanski Franjevci*, I: 132.
26. Ibid., I: 131.
27. Bishop Fra Nikola Ogramić, who has been mentioned before, in 1686 petitioned the Congregatio de Propaganda Fide in Rome for formal permission "to be allowed the use of weapons in war, for it had often happened that he could have shot a few Turks in battle but was not permitted to do so." In 1692 the Province petitioned the Congregation in Rome to absolve a Bosnian Franciscan from an ecclesiastical fine because in defending his monastery he had "killed five Turks" (Batinić, *Djelovanje Franjevaca*, II: 160, 181).

28. Jelenić, *Kultura i Bosanski Franjevci*, II: 264.
29. Jukić, whose activity will be the subject of later discussion in this chapter, reproaches his brethren for being negligent when it came to popular education [*Volksaufklärung*] and for having "learned to love slavery" (*Zemljopis i povjestnica Bosne*, 138). Klaić blames them for having "circumscribed the Catholics too much and made them too servile, thus bringing to naught their national self-confidence" (*Bosna*, 97). Hoernes as well singles out the passivity of the Franciscans with regard to material welfare: "In part the Catholic clergy must shoulder the blame for the long neglect of road building, for with their influence they could have moved material both living and dead" (*Dinarische Wanderungen*, 149).
30. Jukić, *Zemljopis i poviestnica Bosne*, 20; see also Jelenić, *Kultura i Bosanski Franjevci*, II: 100, and Prohaska, *Schrifttum*, 136.
31. Prohaska, *Schrifttum*, 62. Not without interest, though not very convincing either, is the opposite view of those who laid the foundations of literature in Bosnia, held by an anonymous writer: "It was the need arising from within the people itself, not the Reformation, that called forth literary activity in Bosnia. Certainly the writers of that time took for models Catholic works written in answer to the Reformation. But that is all" (*Nada* [Sarajevo, 1897]: 79).
32. Jacobus de Ledesma, *Dottrina christiana breve per insegnar per interrogatione a modo di dialogo* (Rome, 1571); Roberto Bellarmino, *Dottrina christiana breve, composta per ordine di Papa Clemente VIII* (Rome, 1877). See Đorđe S. Đorđević, *Matija Divković. Prilog istoriji Srpske književnosti XVI veka* (Belgrade, 1896–98), 174–78.
33. Rudolf Strohal, *Kratki osvrt na Hrvatsku glagolsku knjigu* (Zagreb, 1912), 53.
34. "And as there was no printing press and there were no letters in our language, I worked with my own hands to create those letters anew and everything else from the ground up." ("Takoier ne budući štampe ni slova ot našega iezika ia moiemi rukami učinih sve koliko iznova i iz temelia svakolika slova.") (from the dedication to *Nauk Krstjanski za narod slovinski* [Venice, 1611]).
35. *Nauk Krstjanski; Sto čudesa aliti zlameniaa blažene i slavne bogorodice, divice Marie* (Venice, 1611).
36. *Nauk Krstjanski s mnoziemi stvari duhovniemi i velebogoljubniemi* (Venice, 1616); *Beside Divkovića svarhu evanjelia nedieljnih [sic]* (Venice, 1616).
37. See Vatroslav Jagić, "Gradja za glagolsku paleografiju," *Rad JAZU* II (Zagreb, 1868): 15, and Jovan Živanović, "Kratak istorijski pregled slova ħ i ђ," *Letopis Matice srpske* 114 (Novi Sad, 1872): 131–36. [Both the dissertation and *Sveske* erroneously cite "p. 114" of this article.—Eds.]

38. Fermendžin, "Acta Bosnae," 321.

39. In 1878 the *Definitorium* issued the following order to the Bosnian Franciscan province: "Omnibus et signulis tam Parochis quam eorum sociis ut dum scribunt litteras sive ad Illm. et Rm. Praesulem sive ad quemcumque allium Praelatum, si vernacula lingua scribunt etiam vernaculis litteris exprimant, non vero ut litteris aliis utantur." And even at the beginning of the nineteenth century the provincial, Dropolić [*sic*], gave strict orders "ut pueros educandos inter alia genera virtutum scribere cyrilice, vulgo sarmski instruant" (*Protocollum Bosnae Argentinae 1739–1835*), in Jelenić, *Kultura i Bosanski Franjevci*, II: 496.

40. Augustin Milletić [*sic*], *Istomačenje stvari potrebitii nauka karstjanskoga* (Rome, 1882 [*sic*]), 6.

41. Stjepan Matijević, *Ispoviedaonik fra Jeronima Panormitana* (Rome, 1630).

42. Pavao Posilović, *Nasladjenie duhovno* (Venice, 1693); *Cviet od kriposti [sic] duhovni i tilesnie* (Venice, 1647).

43. Bartolomeo da Saluthio, *Le sette trombe per risvegliar pecatore a penitenza* (Venice, 1619). [Refers to Cambi.—Eds.]

44. August Vlastelinović, *Pisanka Gospodina Augustina Vlastelinovića iz Sarajeva* (Rome, 1637).

45. Stjepan Markovac, *Ispovid karstjanska* (Venice, 1704); *Fala od Sveti* (Venice, 1708).

46. Fra Ivan Bandulović, *Pisctole i evangelya priko svega godišta* (Venice, 1613).

47. Johannes Anitius, *Speculum sacerdotale (Ogledalo misničko)* (Ancona, 1681), cited in Prohaska, *Schrifttum*, n.p.

48. Johannes Anitius, *Porta caeli et vita aeterna (Vrata nebeska i život vicchni)* (Ancona, 1679), cited in Jelenić, *Kultura i Bosanski Franjevci*, I: n.p.

49. On this see Vatroslav Jagić's review of Tomislav Maretić, *Istorija hrv. pravopisa* in *Archiv für Slavische Philologie* XII (1890): 605.

50. Fra Toma Babić, *Cvit razlika mirisa duhovnoga* (Venice, 1762 [*sic*]).

51. Prohaska, *Schrifttum*, 123.

52. Fra Lovro Sitović, *Pisna od Pakla* (Venice, 1727).

53. Jenenić, *Kultura i Bosanski Franjevci*, I: 144; and Batinić, *Djelovanje Franjevaca*, III: 96.

54. Filippus ab Occhievia [Fra Filip Laštrić], *Epitome Vetustatum Bosniensis Provinciae* (Venice, 1765).

55. Fra Filip Laštrić, *Testimonium billabium seu sermones* (Venice, 1755).

56. Fra Jeronim Filipović, *Pripovi Nauka Krstjanskog* (Venice, 1750). Jelenić knows another edition (Buda, 1769) under the title *Jezgra rimskog pravovirnog Nauka Krstjanskog* (Jelenić, *Kultura i Bosanski Franjevci*, I: 227).

57. Batinić, *Djelovanje Franjevaca,* II: 6–8.
58. On Mrnjavić see Armin Pavić, "Ivan Tomko Mrnjavić," *Rad JAZU* XXXIII (1875): 58–118.
59. Batinić, *Djelovanje Franjevaca,* II: 102.
60. On Gizdelin see Branko Drechsler-Vodnik, "Jura Radojević Gizdelin, knez od Bosne," *Savremenik* IV, no. 3 (1909): 121–27.
61. This trait of religious zeal and near ascetic strictness among the Bosnian Catholics was often observed by all foreigners, especially the apostolic visitors [*visitatoren*]. In 1640 Fra Paolo de Rovigno, serving in that capacity, noted the following: "In questi luoghi habitano christiani divotissimi, come sono anche quelli di tutta Bosna. Gli uomini tutti corrono vegendo il frate a bacciarli la mano, sono tanto devoti, che caminano tutto il giorno per ascoltar la messa" (Zlatović, "Izvještaj o Bosni god. 1640 o. Pavla iz Rovinja," 18). Visitor Ivan de Vietri, who traveled in Bosnia in 1708, maintained that in their life-style the Bosnian Catholics recalled the early Christians: "Non conoscono amoreggiamenti, non suoni, non canti e ne biasteme e se talvolta vogliono divertirsi a cantare cantano Istorie spirituali insegnateli da Religiosi" (in Batinić, "Nekoliko priloga k bosanskoj crkvenoj poviesti," 91–94).
62. Jelenić maintains that in their enthusiasm young Franciscans affixed the Illyrian emblem to gravestones and the walls of churches and monasteries (*Kultura i Bosanski Franjevci,* II: 170–71).
63. Fra Martin Nedić, *Razgovor koga Vile Ilirkinje imadoše u premalitje god 1835.* Fairies (*vilas*) representing the separate Illyrian provinces of Croatia, Dalmatia, Syrmia, etc., hold a meeting for the purpose of spending a happy day entertaining Apollo. The latter, however, is displeased because he misses in the gathering the fairy from Bosnia. This personage appears in the meantime and relates with tear-filled eyes the pangs of her enslavement while the other fairies try to console her.
64. Jelenić, *Kultura i Bosanski Franjevci,* II: 509.
65. Fra Martin Nedić, *Pokret godine 1848 i 1849,* printed by I. Kukuljević in 1851 (Istanbul: Narodna spevanja).
66. *Poraz baša i zavedenje nizama u Bosni* (Pečuj, 1844); *Ratovanje slovinskoga naroda proti Turcima godine 1875–1877* (Dubrovnik, 1881). Under the pseudonym Žalovan.
67. About his school in Varcar, Jukić wrote his friends: "Matters stand as follows with my school in Varcar: Catholic children, 30, including 18 male, 12 female; students of the Serbian Orthodox faith, 17, including 3 married deacons who will soon be ordained into the priesthood" (*Bosanski Prijatelj* [Zagreb, 1850], I: 134). The first school building built by the Franciscans in

which school was held was erected in 1823 by Fra Ilija Starčević in Tolisa. This school was discontinued immediately after his death. Franciscans were in a position to build a larger number of elementary schools only after 1852, when the government in Vienna gave them an annual subvention of 1,500 gulden, at the request of the Bosnian Franciscans, "for building and maintaining Catholic elementary schools." By 1855 there were thirteen and in 1877 thirty-three elementary schools under Franciscan administration (see Jelenić, *Kultura i Bosanski Franjevci*, II: 314–35).

68.   Slavoljub Bošnjak (I. F. Jukić), *Zemljopis i poviestnica Bosne.*
69.   See the monograph by Tugomir Alaupović, *Ivan Franjo Jukić (1818–1857)* (Sarajevo, 1907).
70.   Milena Preindlsberger-Mrazović, ed., *Pjesnička Djela Fra Grge Martića* (Sarajevo, 1893).
71.   Martić, *Zapamćenja*, 59.
72.   Compare Preindlsberger-Mrazović, *Pjesnička Djela*, Introduction, xxiv.
73.   Fra Antun Knežević, *Kratka povjest kralja bosanskih* (Dubrovnik, 1884, 1886, and 1887); *Pad Bosne* (Senj, 1886); *Carsko-turski namjesnici u Bosni i Hercegovini godine 1463–1878.*
74.   See Jelenić, *Kultura i Bosanski Franjevci*, II: 463–68, 481–95, 515–18.
75.   Ibid., II: 433–41, 528–41.
76.   The last person among the Franciscans to make an attempt at bringing the Cyrillic script back into use was Fra Grgo Martić in 1847. At the time he was enthusiastically hailed as "the new Cyril" by Professor Alexander Stojačković of Karlovac. But this attempt foundered and in the end even Martić used the Roman alphabet.
77.   The well-known 1851 ordinance of Omer-Paša ran as follows: "He who is found to be receiving newspapers from foreign Christian countries is to be bound in heavy chains and his entire property forfeited to the state" (Alaupović, *Ivan Franjo Jukić*, 11). "Newspapers and various books were occasionally brought in by carters who concealed them under grain and other kinds of goods and delivered them to the addressees in great fear" (Jelenić, *Kultura i Bosanski Franjevci*, II: 184).

5. The Serbian Orthodox Church

1.   See chapter 3.
2.   Bašagić, *Kratka uputa*, 41.

3. See Konstantin Jireček, "Der Grossvezier Mehmed Sokolović und die serbischen Patriarchen Makarij und Antonij," *Archiv für Slavische Philologie* IX (Berlin, 1886): 291–97.
4. Hudal, *Nationalkirche*, 57.
5. Ibid., 58.
6. Vukičević, *Srpski narod*, 40–41.
7. "This priest from Belgrade, a dyer by profession, learned to read and write in a monastery" (Mijatović, "Pre trista godina," 212).
8. Ibid.
9. Vjekoslav Jelavić, "Kratki francuski putopis kroz Hercegovinu i novopazarski Sandžak iz godine 1614 [*sic*]," *GZM* XIX (1907): 471. [Correct date in title is 1611.—Eds.]
10. Karadžić, *Život i običaji*, 296.
11. Ranke, *Serbien und die Türkei*, 29. An English traveler who stayed for a while in Constantinople at the end of the seventeenth century and had the opportunity of becoming acquainted with the patriarch and his environment wrote as follows: "The power that they have purchased with simony they retain through tyranny. For no sooner do they reach positions of power then they turn immediately to all their bishops to make good the sums expended. Should a bishop try to slip out of it, he is demoted and replaced by someone else. The bishop then pressures the clergy under him, who in turn lean on the people" (George Wheler, *Voyage de Dalmatie, de Grece, et du Levant* [Amsterdam, 1689], n.p.; see Stojan Novaković, "Putničke beleške o balkanskom poluostrvu XVII i XVIII veka," *Godišnica Nikole Čupića* XVII [Belgrade, 1897]: 124). [Andrić refers not to p. 124 but to p. 155 of the article in that volume by Stojan Novaković.—Eds.]
12. Vladimir Ćorović, "Manastir Tvrdoš" [*sic*], *GZM* XXIV (1912): 414. [Not the title of an article in *GZM* by Ćorović; Andrić possibly referred to a subsection of "Hercegovački manastiri," Part II, possibly to Dučić, "Manastiri Duži i Tvrdoš."—Eds.]
13. "The Greek metropolitans ordain as clergy even such people as can hardly read the church books" (Nićifor Dučić, *Istorija srpske pravoslavne crkve od prvijeh desetina VII vijeka do naših dana* [Belgrade, 1892], 202).
14. "They maintained a closer relationship to the supreme secular power than to their own flock" (Ranke, *Serbien und die Türkei*, 29).
15. See chapter 3.
16. See Vatroslav Jagić, "Der erste Cetinjer Kirchendruck vom Jahre 1494," *Denkschriften der Kaiserlichen Akademie der Wissenschaften* XLIII, no. 2 (Vienna, 1894).
17. See Nićifor Dučić, *Književni radovi* I (Belgrade, 1891): 81.

18. See Milan M. Vukičević, "Iz starih Srbulja," *GZM* XIII (1901): 31–70 and 289–350.

19. Ibid., 59 and 303.

20. Prohaska, though he has no proof, is of the opinion that this Biograd is not identical with the modern capital of Serbia but that "Biograd in Hercegovina" is meant (*Schrifttum*, 87). On the other hand, Vuk Stef. Karadžić is inclined to accept that it is today's Serbian capital (*Skupljeni gramatički i polemički spisi* III [Belgrade, 1896]: 381–82). [On p. 89 of his typed dissertation Andrić chose "Belgrad" over "Biograd."—Eds.]

21. Vukičević, "Iz starih Srbulja," 56–57.

22. On the printing of Serbian church books in Romania see Stojan Novaković, "Srpski štampari u Rumuniji," *Godišnica Nikole Čupića* XVII (1897): 331–48. The Wallachian voivode supported the monasteries in Hercegovina not only with church books but by money subsidies (see Vladimir Ćorović, "Hercegovački manastiri: I," *GZM* XXIII [1911]: 510).

23. See Mita Živković, "Srbulje u Sarajevu," *Glasnik Srpskog Učenog Društva* LXIII (Belgrade, 1885): 179–210; and Vukičević, "Iz starih Srbulja," 31–70, 289–350. [Both the dissertation and *Sveske* erroneously cite 209–350. A "srbulja" is a medieval Serbian church book.—Eds.]

24. This note, with which the copyist ended his work, is of unusual interest because it graphically conveys with a few details the patronage of the time and the way church book copying got done: "Being commissioned by lord [*gospodin*] Michael Desisalić and his brothers Nikola and Dragobrat I labored over the writing of this I the sinful and repentent Deacon Mitar and I wrote it in the city of Sarajevo in the house of the reputable Christian and silversmith M. Desisalić who gave me good and cordial hospitality" (Vukičević, "Iz starih Srbulja," 36). [Andrić's original German translation had "Desisavić" for "Desisalić." *Sveske* has provided the original church Slavic source and corrected Andrić accordingly, pp. 232, 233.—Eds.]

25. The copyist of a gospel in the monastery of Sveta Trojica (Plevlje) in the year 1538 closes his work thus: "In these evil and sorrowful times the heartless Turks have thrown themselves on the Christian flock like ravening lions and terror has clouded my understanding so I beg you readers and copyists if anywhere I have erred or miscopied to please in the love of Christ correct me through your good understanding and your learning" (Vukičević, "Iz starih Srbulja," 297). From another gospel belonging to the same monastery and time period: "Sultan Süleyman ruled the Turks during these years and the whole empire was theirs. And they caused us great distress for all we owned they took away from us. Some came while others went and all we had acquired they took away. . . . My

hand is heavy and my understanding is clouded with thinking (worry-ing) about the Turks" (ibid., 313). In the same monastery under the year 1560 the copyist added to a *menaion* [collection of hymns by the month] the usual apology for possible errors: ". . . because I wrote with glazed eyes [*mit gläsernen Augen*] (with eyeglasses?), for I was very old" (ibid.).

26. The following remark is written on a gospel in the Sarajevo church museum: "This happened in the year 1682. The nun Efimia (the name was written in code and only later deciphered) [Andrić interpolation] bought this holy gospel for 30 dinars from a goddamned Turk at the time when our holy monasteries were being destroyed for our sins" (Živković, "Srbulje u Sarajevu," 200). On a manuscript of the homilies of St. John Chrysostom in St. Trojica a notice may be found, dating from 1695: "Herewith let it be known how I, a sinful monk by the name of Zaharija from the Holy Trinity monastery, came and found this book among the children of Ishmael (the Turks) and Novak Besarović bought it from them" (*GZM*, 1901: 291). And on the remnants of another gospel in this same monastery: "This holy book, the Gospel, was in the hands of the Agarenes (Turks). It was saved in the year 1858 on the 13th of November" (Vukičević, "Iz starih Srbulja," 321). See Ljub. Stojanović, "Stari srpski zapisi i natpisi," in *Zbornik za istoriju, jezik i književnost srpskog naroda*, sec. 1, books I, II, III, and X (Belgrade, 1902, 1903, 1908, and 1923). [*Sveske* mistakenly has "IV" for "X."—Eds.]

27. Prohaska, *Schrifttum*, 91.

28. See Ćorović, "Iz dnevnika Prokopije Čokorila," *GZM* XXV: 89–104, 195–207.

29. To leap as Vukičević has done from this fact to the existence of a school is of course risky ("Iz starih Srbulja," 31).

30. Jukić, *Bosanski Prijatelj* I (1850): 132–33.

31. Ivan Ivanić, "Srpske manastirske, seoske i varoške škole u Turskoj," *Godišnjica Nikole Čupića* XXXII (Belgrade, 1913): 195–301.

32. See Klaić, *Poviest Bosne*, 142.

33. See Jelenić, *Kultura i Bosanski Franjevci*, II: 356.

34. This theological school, as also some other schools in Bosnia, was sup-ported by the government in Belgrade. "The schools in Bosnia and Hercegovina, especially the Serbian Orthodox School of Theology in Banja Luka which was founded in the reign of Prince Mihajlo, were subsidized" (Jovan Ristić, *Spoljašnji odnošaji Srbije novijega vremena*, vol. 3 *1868–1872* [Belgrade, 1901], n.p.).

35. Monks were "more richly and more decently clothed and have a better understanding of church rules because they read in church more often,"

etc. (Karadžić, *Život i običaji*, 296); compare also his *Srpski Rječnik* (Vienna, 1852), s.v. "Namastir".

36. See Ćorović, "Hercegovački manastiri," 506–33.

37. "Under Turkish rule the interests of the Serbian people became totally identified with those of the Serbian-Orthodox church" (Jovan N. Tomić, *Deset godina iz istorije srpskog naroda i crkve pod Turcima, 1683–1693* [Belgrade, 1902], 3).

Supplement: The Hybrid Literature of the Bosnian Muslims as an Articulation of Islam's Effect on This Part of the Population

1. Safvetbeg Bašagić alone in Serbo-Croatian literary history attempted to describe the work of Islamic Bosnians in the domain of Islamic literature in a detailed study, "Bošnjaci i Hercegovci u Islamskoj književnosti," *GZM* XXIV (1912): 1–88, 295–390. He managed to assemble the names of over seventy writers who were Bosnians by birth or of Bosnian descent and who contributed in one degree or another to the literature of Islam.

2. Александр Гильфердинг, "Боснія, Герцеговина и старая Сербія," in *Записки Импер. русс. Геогр. Обшества* XIII (St. Petersburg, 1859), reprinted in *Собраніе сочиненій* III (St. Petersburg, 1873).

3. Otto Blau, "Bosnisch-türkische Sprachdenkmäler," *Abhandlungen für die Kunde des Morgenlandes* V, no. 2 (Leipzig: Brockhaus, 1868).

4. Šeh Sejfudin Efendija Kemura and Vladimir Ćorović, *Serbokroatische Dichtungen bosnischer Moslims aus dem XVII, XVIII, und XIX Jahrhundert* (Sarajevo, 1912). On the same topic, see Stojan Novaković, "Srbi Muhamedovci i Turska pismenost," *Glasnik Srpskog Učenog Društva* XXVI (Belgrade, 1869): 220; Friedrich S. Krauss, *Slavische Volksforschungen* (Leipzig: Wilhelm Heims, 1908). [See Novaković, "Prilozi k istoriji srpske književnosti . . ."—Eds.]

Works Cited

The following inventory comprises those works that in the editors' judgment Andrić used in preparing his dissertation. Of the more than 150 sources given in his chapter notes, the majority have been examined *de visu*. One exception is the group of a dozen works by Franciscan writers that had to be verified in Jelenić's compendious history of Catholic culture in Bosnia—the source from which the author himself drew this kind of information, in all likelihood. The fact that otherwise most entries have been taken from actual title pages explains the occasional lack of correspondence in inessential detail between bibliography and notes. Bibliographic information is both more accurate and more copious than that provided by Andrić. Analyzed contents and other comments are directed to readers interested in those of Andrić's readings in history with a direct bearing on his prose fiction.

Alaupović, Tugomir. *Ivan Franjo Jukić (1818–1857)*. Separatni otisak iz dvadesetprvog izvještaja velike gimnazije u Sarajevu. Sarajevo, 1907. 63 pages.
> Basic text of 53 pages, "Život fra Iv. Jukića (Slavoljuba Banjalučanina)," followed by a number of letters from Jukić.

Ančic, Ivan (Johannes Anitius). *Ogledalo misničko*. Ancona, 1681.

———. *Svitlost krstianska i slast duhovna*. Two vols. Ancona, 1679.

———. *Vrata nebeska i život vični*. Two vols. Ancona, 1678.
> Per Marković, Svetozar. *Jezik Ivana Ančića* (Bosanskog pisca xvii veka) (Belgrade, 1958).

Asbóth, Johann von. *Bosnien und die Herzegovina: Reisebilder und Studien*. Vienna, 1888. xii + 488 pages + tables.
> English ed. *An Official Tour through Bosnia and Herzegovina*. London, 1890. 496 pages. Lacks tables. Final chapter in effect an annotated bibliography.

Babić, Fra Toma. *Cvit razlika mirisa duhovnoga*. Venice, 1726.
> Later eds. 1736, 1839 (Dubrovnik), 1849 (Zadar), 1851 (Dubrovnik). 266 pages (I) and 170 pages (II). See Kukuljević Sakcinski, *Arkiv za povjestnicu jugoslavensku* IX (Zagreb, 1868).

Bakula, Petar. *I Martirii nella Missione Francescana Osservante in Ercegovina.* Rome: Tisak Monaldi, 1862.

   Compare Kosir, Fra Vencel, trans. *Hercegovina prije sto godina, ili šematizam fra Petra Bakule. S latinskog originala iz godine 1867 preveo.* . . . Mostar, 1970. 168 pages.

Bandulović, Fra Ivan. *Pisctole i evanghielya priko svega godišta novo istomačena po razlogu Missala Dvora Rimskoga.* Venice, 1613.

Bašagić, Safvet beg. "Bošnjaci i Hercegovci u Islamskoj književnosti." (Pismena radnja za doktorat iz filozofije.) *Glasnik Zemaljskog Muzeja u Bosni i Hercegovini* XXIV (1912): 1–88, 295–390.

   A separate issue, *Bošnjaci i Hercegovci u islamskoj književnosti. Prilog kulturnoj historiji Bosne i Hercegovine,* appeared also the same year in Sarajevo. 184 pages.

———. *Kratka uputa u prošlost Bosne i Hercegovine (od god. 1463–1850).* Sarajevo: Vlastita naklada, 1900.

   Per Bašagić, *Izabrana djela II,* edited by Muhsim Rizvić, Sarajevo, 1971, 255 pages. Andrić refers to this work as "Poviest Bosne." Rizvić's introduction to the first volume of the set observes (p. 49) that it was Bašagić who developed the "thesis that Bosnian Muslims are descendants of the Patarins."

Batinić, Fra Mijo Vjenceslav (bosanski franjevac). *Djelovanje franjevaca u Bosni i Hercegovini za prvih šest viekova njihova boravka.* Vol. I, *Vikarija (1235–1517).* Zagreb, 1881. 155 pages; Vol. II, *Provincija (1517–1699).* Zagreb, 1883. 186 pages; Vol. III, *Provincija (1700–1835).* Zagreb, 1887. 233 pages.

   Chapter headings in the three volumes are as follows:

   I. Osnutak franjevačkog reda.
      Vjerski odnošaji u Bosni prije dolazka franjevaca.
      Prvi franjevci u Bosni.
      Širenje i uspjesi franjevaca.
      Stanje bosanske vikarije za nasliednih borba.
      Sjajno doba bosanke vikarije.
      Franjevci za prve dobe turskoga gospodstva u Bosni.
   II. Prva progonstva (1518–34).
      Razvoj i nevolje bosanske države za dalnje Sulejmanove vladavine (1534–66).
      Nastavak franjevačkih patnja i njihova širenja (1566–96).
      Sudjelovanje franjevaca pri prvom slavonskom ustanku (1596–1610).
      Radinost franjevaca u crkvenih službah (1610–45).
      Franjevci za kandijskog rata (1645–69).
      Propast samostana (1669–83).
      Seoba franjevaca (1683–99).

III. Posliedice karlovačkog mira po bosanske Franjevce (1700–1713).
Nove nutrnje nevolje po franjevce (1714–36).
Potvore (1737–43).
Povod bašaluka i njegove posljedice za Franjevce (1744–57).
Drugi progon (1758–74).
Dalnja nasilja (1775–99).
Nutrnji zapletaji (1800–1812).
Franjevci za posljednjeg jeničarskog brezvladja (1813–35).

―――. *Franjevački samostan u Fojnici od XIV–XX stoljeća*. Zagreb, 1913.

―――. "Njekoliko priloga k bosanskoj crkvenoj poviesti." *Starine* XVII: 77–150. Zagreb, 1885.

Bellarmino, Roberto. *Dottrina cristiana breve, composta per ordine di Papa Clemente VIII*. Rome, 1877. 47 pages.
Andrić refers to the Divković translation, see below: *Istumačenje obilnie nauka karstjanskoga* . . .

Blau, Otto. "Bosnisch-türkische Sprachdenkmäler." *Abhandlungen für die Kunde des Morgenlandes* V, no. 2. Herausgegeben von der Deutschen Morgenländischen Gesellschaft unter der verantwortlichen Redaktion des Prof. Dr. Ludolf Krebl. Leipzig: Brockhaus, 1868. 316 pages.

Bošnjak, Slavoljub. [See Jukić, Ivan Franjo.]

Bulić, Don Fr., and J. Bervaldi. "Kronotaksa solinskih biskupa, uz dodatak: Kronotaksa spljetskih nadbiskupa (od razorenja Solina do polovice XI. v.)." *Bulletino di archeologia e storia dalmata* XXXV (Zagreb, 1912–13). Preštampano iz *Bogoslovske Smotre*, 1912. 180 pages.

Cambi, Bartolomeo da Saluzzo. *Le sette trombe per isvegliare il peccatore à penitenza, et il di lui conforto. Opera utilissima, e di notabile profitto per la salute dell'anime de'peccatori, e peccatrici*. Bassano, 1739.
First ed. Venice, 1619.

Carlerius, Aegidius. "Liber de legationibus concilii Basiliensis pro reductione Bohemorum edente Ernesto Birk." In *Monumenta Conciliorum Generalium seculi decimi quinti. Concilium Basileense. Scriptorum tomus primus*: 359–700. Vienna, 1857.
On the Council of 1433–35.

Ćorović, Vladimir. See Ћоровић, Владимир.

Clemen, O[tto]. See *Libellus de ritu et moribus Turcorum ante LXX annos aeditus, cum prefatione Martini Lutheri*.

Cvijić, Jovan. "Des migrations dans les pays yougoslaves: l'adaptation au milieu." *Revue des Études slaves* III, nos. 1–2: 5–26. Paris, 1923.

Cvit razlika mirisa duhovnoga. [See Babić, Fra Toma.]

Ћоровић, Владимир. "Херцеговачки манастири: I. Требињски манастир (Тврдош)," *GZM* XXIII (1911): 505–33; "II. Дужи;" *GZM* XXIV (1912): 545–53.

————. "Из Дневника Прокопије Чокорила." *GZM* XXV (1913): 89–104, 195–207.

> Contents: I. Омерпашин долазак и влада
>   II. Зулуми Алипашини и турски
>   III. Реформе и њихов утјецај
>   IV. Буне, устанци, борбе с Црногорцима
>   V. Школске и црквене ствари
>   VI. Хроничарске биљешке
>   VII. Биљешке о времену и несрећама

da Saluzzo, Bartolomeo. [See Cambi, Bartolomeo da Saluzzo.]

Divković, Matija. *Beside svarhu evangjelja nediljnieh priko svega godišta.* . . . Venice, 1616.

> Per Jelenić, *Kultura i Bosanski Franjevci,* I: 239.

————. *Istumačenje obilne nauka karstjanskoga, složeno zapovidju O.P.P. Klementa VIII. Od Prisvitloga G. Roberta Bellarmina, Kardinala s. R. C. Prinesena na jazik harvatski zapovidju O.P.P. Urbana VIII.* Rome, 1627.

————. *Nauk karstjanski za narod slovinski.* Venice, 1611.

————. *Nauk karstjanski s mnoziemi stvari duhovniemi i vele bogoljubniemi.* Venice, 1616.

> Six later editions of this popular work are listed by Đorđević in his biography of Matija Divković (see below).

————. *Sto čudesa aliti zlameniaa blažene i slavne bogorodice, divice Marie.* Venice, 1611.

Đorđević, Đorđe S. "Matija Divković. Prilog istoriji Srpske književnosti XVI veka." *Srpska Kraljevska Akademija* LII: 30–139; LIII: 1–135. Belgrade, 1896–98.

> Andrić used a separate edition; see chapter 4, note 32.

Drechsler-Vodnik, Branko. "Jura Radojević Gizdelin, knez od Bosne: crtica iz stare bosanske književnosti." *Savremenik* IV, no. 3 (1909): 121–27.

Дучић, Нићифор. "Историја српске православне цркве од првијех десетина VII вијека до наших дана." In *Књижевни радови Н. Дучића* IX. Belgrade, 1894.

> Per Prohaska, *Schrifttum,* 70.

————. "Манастири Дужи и Тврдош (Требиње) у Херцеговини." In Књижевни радови I. Belgrade, 1891.

Fabianich, Donato. *Firmani inediti dei Sultana di Constantinopoli ai conventi francescani e alle autorità civili di Bosnia e di Erzegovina.* Florence, 1884. 156 pages.

Farlati, Daniele. *Illyrici sacri tomus quartus. Ecclesiae suffraganaae Metropolis Spalatensis.* Venice, 1769.

> Register of the Bosnian bishops, 1141–1740.

Fejér, Georgii. *Codex diplomaticus Hungariae ecclesiasticus ac civilis*. Studio et opera Georgii Fejér, bibliothecarii regii. 10 codices. Vol. I (1382–91). Buda, 1834; Vol. II (1392–1400). Buda, 1834; Vol. III (1352–1400). Buda, 1838; Vol. IV (1401–9). Buda, 1841; Vol. V (1410–17). Buda, 1842.

Fermendžin, P. Eusebius. "Acta Bosnae potissimum ecclesiastica cum insertis editorum documentorum regestis ab anno 925 usque ad annum 1752." *Monumenta Spectantia Historiam Slavorum Meridionalium* XXIII. Zagreb, 1892.

Filipović, Fra Jeronim. *Pripovidagnie nauka karstjanskoga*. Venice, 1750.
　　　Per Jelenić, *Kultura i Bosanski Franjevci*, I: 239.

Filippus ab Occhievia. [See Laštrić, Fra Filip.]

Gjurgjević, Martin. *Memoari sa Balkana (1858–1878)*. Sarajevo, 1910. 195 pages.

Glavaš, R[adoslav]. *Život i rad fra Rafe Barišića*. Mostar, 1900.
　　　Per Prohaska, *Schrifttum*, 184.

Hammer-Purgstall, Joseph. *Des Osmanischen Reichs Staatsverfassung und Staats-verwaltung, dargestelt aus den Quellen seiner Grundgesetze*. 2 vols. Vienna, 1815.
　　　Compare the edition of 1963 by Olms Hildesheim.

Гильфердинг, А. [Hilferding, A.] "Боснія, Герцеговина и старая Сербія." In *Собраніе сочиненій* III. St. Petersburg, 1873. 541 pages.
　　　Contents:
　　　Поездка по Герцеговине, Босніи и старой Сербіи [1857]
　　　Боснія в начале 1858 года
　　　Жизнь Али-Паше Ризванбеговича (Іоалницкія Памучины)
　　　Летопись Босніи 1825–56 (Стаки Скендеревой)
　　　Описаніе монастырей Дужи и Тврдошь в Герцеговине (Н. Дучича)
　　　Летопись Герцеговины 1831–57 (Прокопія Чокорилы)

Hoernes, Moriz. "Alterthümer der Hercegovina." *Sitzungsberichte der philoso-phisch-historische. Classe der kais. Akademie der Wissenschaften* XCVII, no. 2: 491–612. Vienna, 1881.

―――. "Alterthümer der Hercegovina (II) und der südlichen Theile Bos-niens." *Sitzungs-berichte der philosophisch-historische. Classe der kais. Aka-demie der Wissenschaften* XCIX, no. 2: 799–946. Vienna, 1882.

―――. *Dinarische Wanderungen: Cultur- und Landschaftsbilder aus Bosnien und der Herzegovina*. Vienna, 1888. 364 pages.

Hörmann, Kosta. *Narodne pjesne muhamedovaca u Bosni i Hercegovini*. 2 vols. Sarajevo, 1888–89.

Horvat, Karlo. "Monumenta historica nova historiam Bosnae et provinciarum vicinarum illustrantia." *Glasnik Zemaljskog Muzeja u Bosni i Hercegovini* XXI (1909): 1–104, 313–424, 505–17.
　　　Dates on these documents from the Rome archives are 1468–1760.

Hudal, Alois. *Die serbisch-orthodoxe Nationalkirche.* Graz and Leipzig: U. Moser, 1922. vii + 126 pages.

Per National Union Catalogue pre-1956 imprints.

Илијћ [*sic*], Драгутин J. "Српска демократија у средњем веку." Летопис Матице српске 163, no. 3 (1890): 1–28; and 164, no. 4 (1890): 1–47.

Иванић, Иван. "Српске, манастирске, сеоске и варошке школе у Турској, култура српска у Старој Србији и Македонији од XV до XX века." Годишњица Николе Чупића XXXII (1913): 195–301; XXXIII (1914): 305–400. Belgrade. End part two has "свршиће се," but after the war this study was not continued.

Ispoviedaonik, sabran iz pravoslavnieh naučitelja. . . . [See Matijević, Stjepan.]

Jaffé, Philipp; Loewenfeld, S[amuel]; et al. *Regesta pontificum romanorum ab condita ecclesia ad annum post Christum natum 1198, etc.* 2 vols. N. p., 1885–88.

Volume I covers up to A.D. 1138, volume II thence to 1198.

Jagić, Vatroslav. "Der erste Cetinjer Kirchendruck vom Jahre 1494. Eine bibliographisch-lexikalische Studie. I. Hälfte: Bibliographisch-Kritisches. (Mit 1 Tafel.)" *Denkschriften der Kaiserlichen Akademie der Wissenschaften* XLIII, no. 2: 1–80. Vienna, 1894.

———. "Gradja za glagolsku paleografiju." *Rad Jugoslavenske Akademije Znanosti i Umjetnosti* II: 1–35. Zagreb, 1868.

———. "Istorija hrvatskoga pravopisa latinskim slovima. Napisao Dr. T. Maretić (Zagreb, 1889), 406 pp." in *Archiv für Slavische Philologie* XII (1890): 602–9.

———. "Nekoliko riječi o bosanskim natpisima na stećcima." *Glasnik Zemaljskog Muzeja u Bosni i Hercegovini* II: 1–9. Sarajevo, 1890.

Jastrebov, I. "Sadržaj fermana koje je izradilo sebi katoličko sveštenstvo kod porte o svom odnošaju prema pravoslavnom mitropolitu hercegovačkom i bosanskom." *Glasnik Srpskog Učenog Društva* XLVIII: 405–18. Belgrade, 1880.

Jelavić, Vjekoslav. "Kratki francuski putopis kroz Hercegovinu i novopazarski Sandžak iz godine 1611." *Glasnik Zemaljskog Muzeja u Bosni i Hercegovini* XIX (1907): 471–82.

Jelenić, Julian. *Kultura i Bosanski Franjevci.* Vol. I. Sarajevo, 1912. 256 pages; Vol. II. Sarajevo, 1915. 603 pages.

———. *Ljetopis franjevačkog samostana u Kreševu.* Sarajevo, 1918. (Originally published in *Glasnik Zemaljskog Muzeja u Bosni i Hercegovini* XXIX: 1–95 [1917].)

Covers the years 1765–99. In Latin. Includes glossary of Turkisms, index of names.

Jireček, Constantin. "Der Grossvezier Mehmed Sokolović und die serbischen

Patriarchen Makarij und Antonij. (Zur Tekstkritik und Interpretation der serbischen Annalen.)" *Archiv für Slavische Philologie* IX: 291–97. Berlin, 1886.

———. "Staat und Gesellschaft im mittelalterlichen Serbien. Studien zur Kulturgeschichte des 13.–15. Jahrhunderts." *Denkschriften der kaiserlichen Akademie der Wissenschaften. Philosophisch-Historische Klasse* LVI, no. 2 (part I): 1–83; and no. 3 (part II): 1–74. Vienna, 1912.

Jukić, I[van] F[ranjo] Banjalučanin, ed. *Bosanski Prijatelj: časopis saderžavajući potriebite koristne i zabavne stvari.* Vol. I. Zagreb, 1850.

———. [Bošnjak, Slavoljub]. *Zemljopis i poviestnica Bosne.* Zagreb: Berzotiskom narodne tiskarnice Ljudevita Gaja, 1851. 164 pages.

Капетановић, Мехмед-бег. *Народно благо. Сакупио и издао Мехмед-бег Капетановић-Љубушак по Босни, Херцеговини и сусједним Крајевима. Додатак: Превод неких арапских, персијских и турских пословица и мудрих изрека.* Sarajevo, 1888. 396 pages.

Karadžić, Vuk Stef. *Skupljeni gramatički i polemički spisi.* Državno izdanje, knjiga III. Belgrade, 1896.

———. *Srpske narodne pjesme.* 2d ed. Drugo državno izdanje. Knjiga druga, u kojoj su pjesme junačke najstarije. Belgrade, 1895.

———. *Srpski Rječnik, istumačen njemačkijem i latinskijem riječima.* Vienna, 1852.

———. *Život i običaji naroda srpskoga.* Vienna, 1867.

Kemura, Šeh Sejfudin Efendija. "Iz Sejahatname Evlije Čelebije." *Glasnik Zemaljskog Muzeja u Bosni i Hercegovini* XX (1908): 183–201, 289–341. (Sejahatnama "travel notes" [Turk.].)

———, and Vladimir Čorovič. "Прилози за хисторију православне цркве у Босни и Херцеговини у XVIII. i XIX. стољећу." *G.Z.M.* XXIV (1912). 413–41.

Documents from 1763 through 1860.

———. *Serbokroatische Dichtungen bosnischer Moslims aus dem XVII, XVIII, und XIX Jahrhundert.* Sarajevo, 1912. xxviii + 75 pages.

Kidrič, Franz. *Bartolomaeus Georgijević: Biographische und bibliographische Zusammenfassung.* Vol. II of *Mitteilungen des Muzeion im Auftrag des Verlages Ed. Strache.* Vienna, 1920.

Klaić, Vjekoslav. *Bosna. Podatci o zemljopisu i poviesti Bosne i Hercegovine.* Poučna knjižica "Matice Hrvatske," vol. III. Zagreb, 1878. 222 pages.

———. *Poviest Bosne do propasti kraljevstva.* Zagreb, 1882. 352 pages.

Knežević, Antun. *Carsko-turski namjestnici u Bosni-Ercegovini godine 1463–1878.* Senj, 1887. 93 pages.

Per British Museum listing.

———. "Kako se zemlje u Bosni diele." *Bosanski Prijatelj* IV. Zagreb, 1870.

Per Jelenić, *Kultura i Bosanski Franjevci,* II: 444–45.

————. *Pad Bosne*. Senj, 1886. 107 pages.

————. Per Jelenić, *Kultura i Bosanski Franjevci*, II: 480.

Knežević, O. Antun [Bošnjak iz Varcara, R.S.O. Franc Asizskoga]. *Kratka povjest kralja bosanskih. Po izvorima napisao za mladež bosansku—*. Volume I (Narodna biblioteka, knjiga XVII), Dubrovnik, 1884. vi + 75 pages.

Koetschet. Dr. Josef K. *Osman Pascha, der letzte grosse Wesier Bosniens, und seine Nachfolger*. Sarajevo, 1909. 87 pages.

> See also the earlier book by Koetschet [1830–98], *Aus Bosniens Letzter Türkenzeit*, Vienna, 1905, which covers the action of Andrić's 1925 story, "Mara, milosnica."

Krauss, Friedrich S. *Slavische Volkforschungen. Abhandlungen über Glauben, Gewohnheitrechte, Sitten, Bräuche und die Guslarenlieder der Südslaven*. Leipzig: Wilhelm Heims, 1908. 431 pages.

Krauss, F. S., and J. Duimo Beckmann. "Über den Einfluss des Orients auf die Südslaven." *Das Ausland. Wochenschrift für Länder- und Völkerkunde*. Nos. 14: 261–64; 15: 185–288; 16: 308–12; and 17: 330–32. Stuttgart and Munich, April 1887.

Kreševljaković, Hamdija. *Kratak pregled hrvatske knjige u Herceg-Bosni od najstarijih vremena do danas*. Sarajevo, 1912. 53 pages.

Kuripešić, Benedikt. [See Matković, Petar.]

Kukuljević-Sakcinski, Ivan, ed. *Arhiv za povjestnicu jugoslovensku* IX. Zagreb, 1868.

Laštrić, Fra Filip [Filippus ab Occhievia]. *Epitome Vetustatum Bosnensis Provinciae*. Venice, 1765. 48 pages.

————. *Testimonium bilabium seu sermones panegyrico-dogmatico morales pro solemnitatibus D. Sabaoth latine et illyrice elaborati*. Venice, 1755.

Ledesma, Jacobus de. *Dottrina christiana breve per insegnar per interrogatione a modo di dialogo*. Rome, 1571.

> Compare Laurence Vaux. *A catechisme or Christian doctrine*, vol. 280 [147]. 39 pages. [English recusant literature, 1558–1640, vol. 2.]

Levy, Moritz. *Die Sephardim in Bosnien: Ein Beitrag zur Geschichte der Juden auf der Balkanhalbinsel. Mit 29 Illustrationen im Tekste*. Sarajevo: Daniel A. Kajon, 1911. 127 pages.

Libellus de ritu et moribus Turcorum ante LXX annos aeditus, cum prefatione Martini Lutheri. Wittemberg: Iohann Lufft, 1530. 175 pages.

> Also called Tractatus (de ritu, etc.). Memorandum card in Harvard University Library reads: "This work, wrongly attributed to Georgius de Hungaria (Bartolomej Georgević) by confusion with his *De Turcarum moribus*, was written by an unknown Transylvanian who was a captive in Turkey about the middle of the fifteenth century. It was published

under many different titles during the fifteenth and sixteenth centuries. . . ."

Maretić, T[omislav]. *Istorija hrvatskoga pravopisa latinskijem slovima*. Djela Jugoslavenska Akademija Znanosti i Umjetnosti IX. Zagreb, 1889. 403 pages. Reprinted as *Istorija hrv. pravopisa* in *Archiv für Slavische Philologie* XII (1890). 605 pages.

Markovac [Margitić], Stjepan. *Fale od sveti, alliti govorenjia od svetkovima, zabilježeni priko godišta. Takoier govorenjia svarhu evangjelja, u sve nedilje priko godišta*. Venice, 1708.

Per Jelenić, *Kultura i Bosanski Franjevci*, I: 239.

———. *Izpovied karstianska, i nauk znati se pravo izpoviditi urešena s mnogim stvarima duhovnim, i prilikam izvagjeno iz razliki knjiga latinski, veoma korisno*. Venice, 1701.

Per Jelenić, *Kultura i Bosanski Franjevci*, I: 230.

Martić, Fra Grgo. *Zapamćenja (1829–1878)*. Zagreb, 1906.

The following note appears in Kecmanović, *Fra Grgo Martić: Izabrani spisi*, p. 281: "Po kazivanju autorovom zabilježio Janko Koharić. Za tisak priredio Ferdo Šišić. U Zagrebu, nakladom Gjure Trpinca, tiskara, 1906. Str. viii + 119 pages + (na str. pred nasl. listom) fotogr. Fra Grge Martića. (Na poledjini nasl. lista): Faksimil autografa: Ovi Brzopis bilježen bješe po mojemu ustmenomu kazivanju od Gospodina brzopisca Janka Koharića iz Zagreba u Samostanu Kreševu d. 15 kolovoza 1901. F. G. Martić."

Matijević, Stjepan, trans. *Ispovjednik fra Jeronima Panormitana*. Rome, 1630.

Per Jelenić, *Kultura i Bosanski Franjevci*, I: 229.

Matković, Petar. "Putovanja po balkanskom poluotoku XVI vieka. II. Putovanja B. Kuripešića, L. Nogarola, B. Ramberta." *Rad Jugoslavenske Akademije Znanosti i Umjetnosti* LVI: 141–232. Zagreb, 1881.

Mijatović, Čedomilj. "Pre trista godina. Prilog k izučavanju izvora za istoriju našeg naroda u XVI-om veku." *Glasnik Srpskog Učenog Društva* XXXVI: 155–219. Zagreb, 1872.

The trips through Serbia of one Gerlach, 1573 and 1578, probably the first Protestant to travel there. Andrić very closely paraphrases the mechanics of the Adžami-Oglan herein described.

Miklošić, Fr[anz], ed. *Monumenta Serbica spectantia historiam Serbiae Bosnae Ragusii*. Vienna, 1858. 580 pages.

Miletić, Augustin. *Istumačenje stvari potrebitih nauka krstjanskoga za uvižbanje dice i čeljadi priprostite u državi bosanskoj*. Rome, 1828.

Per Prohaska, *Schrifttum*, 145. Both Andrić and *Sveske* have 1882.

Murko, Matthias. *Das Serbische Geistesleben*. Leipzig and Munich: Süddeutsche Monatshefte, 1916. 53 pages.

Nedić, Fra Martin. *Stanje Redodržave Bosne Srebrene poslje pada kraljevstva Bosan-skog pak do okupacije.* Gjakovo, 1884.
    Per Jelenić, *Kultura i Bosanski Franjevci,* I: 185; and Kreševljaković, *Kratak pregled hrvatske knjige,* 28.

———. (Martić Žalovan i njegov brat Bošnjak). *Pokret godine 1848 i 1849.* Istanbul: Narodna spevanja, 1851. 126 pages.
    Per Kukuljević Sakcinski, *Arhiv* and also *Bibliografija Hrvatska, dio prvi,* Zagreb, 1860. Jelenić explains that Kukuljević himself published the above work at his own expense (II: 510). The second author was Fra Marijan Šunjić, whose pseudonym was also "Žalovan."

———. *Poraz baša i zavedenje nizama u Bosni.* Pečuj, 1844.
Njegoš, Petar II Petrović. *Gorski vijenac.* 8th ed. Belgrade, 1923.
Novaković, Stojan. "Burkard i Bertrandon de-la-Brokijer o Balkanskom Pol-uostrvu XIV i XV veka." *Godišnjica Nikole Čupića* XIV: 1–66. Belgrade, 1894.

———. "Prilozi k istoriji srpske književnosti, IV: Srbi Muhamedovci i Turska pismenost. (Na osnovu knjige: *Bosnisch-Türkische Sprachdenkmäler, gesam-melt, gesichtet und herausgegeben von Dr. Otto Blau,* Leipzig, 1868)." *Glasnik Srpskog Učenog Društva* IX, no. 26 (old series): 220–55. Belgrade, 1869.

———. "Путничке белешке о балканском полуострву XVII и XVIII века." Годишњица Николе Чупића, XVII: 73–165. Belgrade, 1897.
    This work is in five parts, as follows:

    I. Account by John Burbury, member of a delegation traveling in the Balkans 1665–66, printed London 1671. Pages 73–99.

    II. Description of Turkey by an unknown Russian prisoner dating from the second half of the seventeenth century (between 1672 and 1686) and published in Russia in 1890. Pages 100–112.

    III. Journey of the English scientist George Wheler in 1675–76, follow-ing the French translation of 1689. Pages 113–35.

    IV. Notes by the Turkish traveler Evlija-Efendi, mid-seventeenth cen-tury, which had been published by Hammer in London, 1846 and 1850. Of interest for its list of Turkish notables who were of Balkan Slavic origin, or else of Albanian derivation. Pages 136–44.

    V. Unpublished manuscript notes of the French ambassador to the Porte, one St.-Priest, including his trip to Belgrade of 1768 and return to Carigrad [Istanbul]. Diary entries 22 Sept.–13 Nov. 1768. Pages 145–65.

———. *Srbi i Turci XIV i XV veka. Istorijske studije o prvim borbama c najezdom Turskom pre i posle boja na Kosovu.* Isdanje Čupićeve Zadužbine XXXIII. Belgrade: Državna Štamparija, 1893. vii + 397 pages.
    Listed in "Spisak izdanja zadužbine Nikole Čupića 1875–1940." *Godiš-njica Nikole Čupića* L: p. 206, item 33. Belgrade, 1941. Including the

German translation of 1898, there have been three subsequent editions of this important work.

———. "Srbi Muhamedovci i Turska pismenost." See his "Prilozi k istoriji srpske kniževnosti, IV."

———. "Srpski štampari u Rumuniji: Beleške." *Godišnjica Nikole Čupića* XVII: 331–48. Belgrade, 1897.

Pavić, Armin. "Ivan Tomko Mrnavić." *Rad Jugoslavenske Akademije Znanosti i Umjetnosti* XXXIII: 58–127. Zagreb, 1875.

Pavlinović, Mihovil. *Puti. (Godine 1867–75.)* Zadar, 1888.

> Published first in fragments in the periodicals, later as a whole in *Narodni list.* The 1888 edition is posthumous. Part 2 deals with Bosnia in 1874. Pavlinović, who liked to travel in the guise of a village doctor, had earlier described an 1856 trip to Vienna by way of Trieste. Compare Andrić's characteristic genre of *putopisi.*

Pisctole i evanghielya priko svega godišta. . . . [See Bandulović, Fra Ivan.]

Попруженко, М. Г., ed. "Св. Козмы Пресвитера Слово на Еретики и Поучение отъ Божественныхъ книгъ." Памятники Древней Письменности и Искусства CLXVII. St. Petersburg: Типография И. Н. Скороходова (Надеждинская 43), 1907. xiv + 86 pages.

Posilović, Pavao. *Cviet od koristih duhovni i tilesnie, izvaden iz jezika latinskoga u jezik ilirički aliti slovinski.* Venice, 1647.

> Per Jelenić, *Kultura i Bosanski Franjevci,* I: 229.

———. *Naslagjenje duhovno koi želi dobro živiti, potomtoga umriti i ponukovati osugjene na smrt od pravde. Jedan karstianin kako immase ispoviditi, i svoju dušu po razlogu izkušati i pristupiti kispovidniku. Iošte mnoge molitve, i salone, i ostale stvari veoma potrebite i t. d.* Venice, 1682.

> Per Jelenić, *Kultura i Bosanski Franjevci,* I: 229. Andrić used an edition of 1693.

Preindlsberger-Mrazović, Milena, ed. *Pjesnička Djela Fra Grge Martića.* Sarajevo, 1893.

Prelog, Milan. *Povijest Bosne u doba osmanlijske vlade.* Vol. 1, *1463–1739;* Vol. 2, *1739–1878.* Sarajevo: Naklada J. Studničke i druga, n.d. 178 and 190 pages, respectively.

> A survey written sometime between 1911 (latest dated footnote) and 1926 (when acquired by Harvard library). No contents, no bibliography. Note chapters on *"Geistliches Leben."*

Pripovidagnie nauka karstjanskoga. [See Filipović, Fra Jeronim.]

Prohaska, Dragutin. *Das kroatisch-serbische Schrifttum in Bosnien und der Herzegowina von den Anfängen im XI. bis zur nationalen Wiedergeburt im XIX. Jahrhundert.* Zagreb, 1911. viii + 202 pages + map.

Pucić, Medo. *Spomenici Srъbski od 1395 do 1423, to jest Pisma pisana od Republike*

Dubrovačke Kraljevima, Despotima, Vojvodama i Knezovima, Srъbskiem, Bo-sanskiem i Primorskiem. Belgrade, 1858. xxxvii + 177 pages + xxxi.

Rački, Franjo. "Bogomili i Patareni." *Rad Jugoslavenske Akademije Znanosti i Umjetnosti* VII (Zagreb, 1869): 84–179; VIII (1869): 121–87; X (1870): 160–263.

————, ed. *Documenta Historiae Chroaticae Periodum Antiquam [sic] illustrantia.* Monumenta Spectantia Historiam Slavorum Meridionalium, vol. VII. Zagreb, 1877. xxxv + 544 pages.

Consists of Acta, Rescripta, and Synodalia, in two major sections, detailed index, and (in front matter) a chronology from first appearance of the Slavs with Avars A.D. 548–611 to 1100, each entry keyed to page in the text.

————. "Prilozi za povjest bosanskih Patarena." *Starine* I: 93–140. Zagreb: Jugoslavenska Akademija Znanosti i Umjetnosti, 1869.

————. "Prilozi za zbirku srbskih i bosanskih listina." *Rad Jugoslavenske Akademije Znanosti i Umjetnosti* I: 124–63. Zagreb, 1867.

————, ed. *Thomas archidiaconus: Historia Salonitana.* In *Scriptores,* vol. 3 of Monumenta Spectantia Historiam Slavorum Meridionalium, vol. XXVI. Zagreb, 1894. 225 pages.

Edition of a manuscript from the Split archives dating from end of the thirteenth–beginning of the fourteenth centuries. (Thomas d. 1266.)

Ranke, Leopold von. *Serbien und die Türkei in XIX Jahrhundert.* Vols. 43 and 44 of his *Collected Works.* Leipzig, 1879. 558 pages.

Contents: I. History of Serbia to 1838
   II. Bosnia in relation to the reforms of Sultan Mahmud II (pp. 287–333)
   III. 1839–41
   IV. Serbia under the European powers since 1842

Rigler, Lorenz. *Die Türkei und deren Bewohner in ihren naturhistorischen, physiologischen und pathologischen Verhältnissen vom Standpunkte Constantinopels.* Geschildert von —, k.k. österreichischem Professor, derzeit Lehrer der med. Klinik an der Schule zu Constantinopel. 2 vols. Vienna, 1852.

Details of flora, fauna, health care, bathing, use of drugs, acclimatization of foreigners to the Orient, diseases and medicines, hospitals, and (p. 186) dietary customs. Part 2 (p. 58) describes *Lichen,* a fungus growth on the skin, and its cure or alleviation by rubbing with a salve (*Oleum jecoris Aselli*). Compare Veli Pasha in "Mara, milosnica."

Ristić, Jovan. *Spoljašnji odnošaji Srbije novijega vremena.* Vol. 3, *1868–1872.* Belgrade, 1901. 352 pages.

Chapter 6 (pp. 119–202) concerns Austro-Hungary and the Bosnian question.

Volumes I (1848–60) and II (1860–68) published in 1887.

Rośkiewicz, Johann (k.k. Major im Generalstube). *Studien über Bosnien und die Hercegovina. Mit elf Abbildungen in Holzschnitt und einer lithographirten Karte.* Leipzig and Vienna, 1868. 424 pages.

Ruvarac, Ilarion. *O humskim episkopima i hercegovačkim mitropolitima do godine 1766.* Otštampano iz knjige "Srpska pravoslavna herz.-zahumska mitro-polija pri kraju 1900 god." 31 pages.

> Per Nikola Radojčić, "Spisak radova Ilariona Ruvarca" in *Spomenica Ilarionu Ruvarcu,* Novi Sad, 1955, p. 160. Same article in *Glas Srbske kralj. Akad.* LXII, 1901, under title "Рашки епископи и митрополити; од архимандрита И. Р." 46 pages.

Sitović, Fra Lovro. *Pisna od Pakla—navlastito od paklenoga ognja, tamnosti i vič-nosti, koju iz Svetoga pisma i novoga zakona; takodjer iz svetih otaca i naučitelja izvede.* Venice, 1727.

> Per Prohaska, *Schrifttum,* 136.

Skarić, Vlad. "Jedna naredba o rajinom odijelu iz doba otomanske vladavine." *Glasnik Zemaljskog Muzeja u Bosni i Hercegovini* XIV (1902): 557–59.

Stojanović, Ljub. "Stare Srpske Štamparije." *Srpski Književni Glasnik* VII, no. 3, 4, 5, and 6. Belgrade, 1902.

———. "Stari srpski zapisi i natpisi." In *Zbornik za istoriju, jezik i književnost srpskoga naroda.* Section 1, books I, II, III, and X. Belgrade, 1902, 1903, 1908, and 1923.

> Contents: I. Datable records and inscriptions from the twelfth century to 1700. 480 pages.
>
> II. Inscriptions and other approximately datable materials, 1701–1892. 482 pages.
>
> III. Indexes.
>
> X. Materials approximately datable 996–1700. 227 pages.

Strohal, Rudolf. *Kratki osvrt na hrvatsku glagolsku knjigu.* Zagreb, 1912. 243 pp.

> On the Glagolithic priests of the twelfth to nineteenth centuries, their lives and education, categories of books in the Glagolithic script, lists of names, and their dates.

Strukić, Ign[acije]. *Povjestničke crtice Kreševa i franjevačkog samostana.* Sarajevo, 1899.

> Per Jelenić, *Kultura i Bosanski Franjevci,* II: 6, passim; Kreševljaković, *Kratak pregled hrvatske knjige,* 25, 47.

Šafarik, Janko. "Srbski istorijski Spomenici Mletačkog arhiva. Prepisao—. Monumenta Historica Serbica Archivi Veneti." *Гласникъ Друштва Србс-ке Словесности* XI. Belgrade, 1859.

> The *Друштво Србске Словесности* was reconstituted in 1865 as the *Србско учено друштво,* the first issue of its journal becoming volume 18 of the old series, which had been published from 1841.

Thallóczy, Ludwig von. [Ljudevit p. Dr.] *Studien zur Geschichte Bosniens und*

Serbiens im Mittelalter. Translated by Franz Eckhart. Munich and Leipzig, 1914. 478 pages.

Studies of Bosnian and Hercegovinian royal families in the 1400s.

Theiner, Augustin. *Vetera monumenta historica Hungariam sacram illustrantia maximam partem nondum edita ex tabulariis Vaticans deprompta collecta ac serie chronologica disposita, ab—*. Vol. I (1216–1352). Rome, 1859; Vol. II (1352–1526). Rome, 1860.

In volume I Andrić refers to documents, not pages (contra his notes), e.g. Nos. 373, 374, p. 202. In volume II he refers to pages.

———. *Vetera monumenta Slavorum Meridionalium historiam illustrantia.* Vol. I. Rome, 1863.

Per John Fine, *The Bosnian Church, East European Quarterly,* 1975, p. 400.

Tomić, Jovan N. *Deset godina iz istorije srpskog naroda i crkve pod Turcima, 1683–1693.* Belgrade, 1902. 136 pages [?].

Per Jovan Tomitch, *Les Albaniens,* 1913, p. 33n.

Truhelka, Ćiro. "Bosanska vlastela srednjeg vijeka." *Nada* (Sarajevo, 1901). (The periodical *Nada* could not be located in U.S. libraries.)

———. *Die geschichtliche Grundlage der bosnischen Agrarfrage.* Sarajevo, 1911.

A separate issue, enlarged, of this small study appeared in 1915 published by the *Glasnik Zemaljskog Muzeja,* Sarajevo, 110 pages.

———. "Gazi Husrefbeg, njegov život i njegovo doba." *Glasnik Zemaljskog Muzeja u Bosni i Hercegovni* XXIV, no. 1 (1912): 91–232. Sarajevo.

———. "Tursko-slovjenski spomenici dubrovačke arhive." *Glasnik Zemaljskog Muzeja u Bosni i Hercegovni* XXIII (1911): 1–62, 303–50, 437–84. Sarajevo.

Per Fine, *The Bosnian Church,* p. 432. Documents the years 1430–1542. Separately issued as book in 1911, 258 pages, with nineteen facsimiles. See Prelog, *Povijest Bosne,* p. 10n.

Veselinović, M. V. "Esnafi u Skoplju (Iz povećeg sastava o Skoplju koji spremam za štampu)." *Godišnjica Nikole Čupića* XV: 223–42. Belgrade, 1895.

Властелиновић, Аугустин. Писанка из Сарајева сложена на част и почтение присвитлом г. Јеролиму Луцићу, Варешанину бискупу дриватскому владаотцу босанскому, скрадинскому и посавскому, стрицу свому пољубљеному. Rome, 1637.

Per Prohaska, *Schrifttum,* 109.

Vrčević, Vuk. *Narodne pripovijesti i presude iz života po Boki Kotorskoj, Hercegovini i Crnogori.* Dubrovnik, 1890. 278 pages.

Per Radmila Pešić, *Vuk Vrčević.* Filološki Fakultet Beogradskog Univerziteta. Monografie XIV. Belgrade, 1967. P. 208.

Vukasović, Vid Vuletić. *Bilježke o kulturi južnih Slavena, osobito Srbalja.* Dubrovnik, 1899.

Вукичевић, Милан М. "Из старих Србуља. (Са 21 сликом у тексту)." *Г.З.М.* XIII (1901): 31–70, 289–350.

————. *Српски народ, црква и свештенство у турском царству од 1459–1557 год.* Belgrade, 1896.

Per Prohaska, *Schrifttum*, 70.

Waddingus, Luca Hibernus. *Annales Minorum seu Trium Ordinum a S. Francisco institutorum.* 2d ed. Rome, 1731.

Weingart, Miloš. "Počátky bogomilství, prvního opravného hnutí u Slovanu." *Slovanský Přehled: sborník statí, dopisuv a zpráv ze života slovanského* XVI: 6–19. Prague: F. Šimáček, 1914.

Wheler, George. *Voyage de Dalmatie, de Grece, et du Levant. Enrichi de Medailles, & de Figures des principales Antiquitez qui se trouvent dans ces lieux, avec la Description des Coutumes, des Villes, Rivieres, Ports de Mer, & de ce qui s'y trouve de plus remarquable. Traduit de l'Anglois.* 2 vols. Amsterdam, 1689.

Andrić's reference to Wheler's journey is to page 155 of volume I of the above French translation, as he found it reproduced by Stojan Novaković in "Putničke beleške o balkanskom poluostrvu XVII i XVIII veka."

Zlatović, Stipan. "Izvještaj o Bosni god. 1640 o. Pavla iz Rovinja." *Starine* XXIII: 1–38. Zagreb, 1890.

Žalovan [Fra Martin Nedić]. *Ratovanje slovinskoga naroda proti Turcima godine 1875–1877.* Dubrovnik, 1881. 168 pages.

Per Jelenić, *Kultura i Bosanski Franjevci*, II: 510.

Živanović, Jovan. "Kratak istorijski pregled slova ђ i ћ." *Letopis Matice srpske* 114: 131–36. Novi Sad, 1872.

Живковић, Мита. "Србуље у Сарајеву, I до XIV." *Гласник Српскога ученог друштва* LXIII: 179–220. Belgrade, 1885.

Index

About the Editors

Želimir B. Juričić is Professor and Chair of the Slavonic Studies Department at the University of Victoria, British Columbia, and author of *Ivo Andrić: Letters, The Man and the Artist: Essays on Ivo Andrić,* and *Ivo Andrić u Berlinu 1939–1941.*

John F. Loud is Associate Professor of Russian and Latin at Texas Christian University and translator of Milovan Djilas, *Rise and Fall* (1985).